Star Chambers
The Race For Fusion Power

by Melanie Windridge

Edited by Mark Griffith 2012

First published April 2012 by White Label Books, an
imprint of Moving Toyshop Publishing,
278 Manor Avenue, Sale, Cheshire, M33 4NB

Typeset in Arno Pro Display and Helvetica Neue by
Regina Racz, Budapest, Hungary

Printed and bound in the UK by
Butler Tanner & Dennis Ltd
Frome

ISBN 978-1-907913-50-1

Star Chambers
The Race For Fusion Power

by Melanie Windridge

Contents

Week 1 Why We Need Fusion

This book is adapted from a weblog I wrote while travelling round Britain, talking to students about fusion physics.

Nuclear fusion has been tantalising us with its promise for half a century. It creates only short-lived radioactive waste, yields vastly more energy than any other source, and the fuel it burns is far far cheaper than uranium or even coal. It's clean, abundant, and very cheap. Fusion is after all the power that keeps our very own Sun burning for millions of years.

But this is the one thing that makes fusion power such a challenge - what do you make your power station out of to hold something as hot as the insides of a star? Learning to generate fusion power means learning to build star chambers...

...but I'm getting ahead of myself - back to week one on my tour of Britain.

This year, 2010, I am the Schools and Colleges Lecturer for the Institute of Physics (IoP). The IoP runs an annual tour, with a lecturer visiting around 35 schools to deliver a talk on a particular aspect of physics. This year that lecturer is me, and I am going to be talking about "Powering the Future – the Physics behind Fusion". As I go along, I'm going to try and keep you updated about my movements around the country, and also give you a little, bite-size chunk of fusion info to take away with you each time.

I arrived in Crawley on Sunday evening. I had a hotel booked as I had an early talk at the school the next morning. It was dark and drizzly as I negotiated the multiple road closures in the centre of town and wished I had a satnav. I wiggled through the tight roads of an estate until, incongruous, my hotel loomed large as I rounded a bend. I checked in and found my room: clean, modern. The only drawback was a disappointing lack of biscuits.

I reached the school an hour early at 8.30am to set up my equipment. Later the children arrived in class groups and the lecture theatre was packed – students even sat on the floor at the front. The school said we had about 240 people – a mixture of years 10, 11, and some sixth form. They were calm and seemed to enjoy the talk. Plenty of volunteers helped, and people asked lots of interesting questions at the end, including one boy asking what qualifications he would need to work in fusion. Quite a satisfying end!

So, onto our bite-sized chunk of fusion info. Since it's day one, we'll just have a think about what fusion is and why we need it. Let's first of all think about what the word "fusion" means - it means the joining together of two or more things to form a single entity. We'll be talking about nuclear fusion, that is fusing the nuclei of atoms together.

Now I want you to imagine that you are lying outside, sunbathing on a really hot day. I want you to feel the warmth of the Sun on your face – all that energy. Now imagine the Sun itself. The Sun is a huge ball of plasma and it is undergoing fusion reactions to sustain itself, because nuclear fusion is the reaction that powers the Sun and stars. And now I want you to imagine all the tiny particles inside the Sun. They're all zooming around in different directions, some of them are colliding with each other and fusing, and when they fuse they release energy – that energy that you feel.

Now I want you to imagine reaching out and taking a little piece of that sunshine and bringing it down to Earth, because we want to use it to make clean energy for mankind. But we have a problem. Because without the huge mass of the Sun, without all that gravitational pressure, our little piece of sunshine is escaping and cooling. So we need to find some way of keeping it trapped. But it's the Sun – it's really hot – so we can't just put it in a box. We need to find some other way of containing it.

What we do is build something called a tokamak, a machine like that illustrated on the last page of this chapter. I'm going to tell you more about these machines, these tokamaks, as we go along, but for the time being I just want to give you an idea of the size and scale of these machines. Look for the workman in the picture, to get an idea of the size of JET – the largest tokamak in the world. You can see from that illustration that fusion machines are huge, and fusion really is a massive undertaking.

Fusion as an energy source would solve the major world energy problems that are beginning to arise today. We are in the middle of an energy crisis. We have the problems of finite fossil fuels and energy security. Even as energy companies search for new reserves and employ ever-more-expensive extraction techniques we know that, one day, those reserves of oil, gas, and coal will run out. We also want to be sure that we have access to the energy resources that we need, while at the moment much of the world's energy supplies, fossil fuels, are located in relatively

Reverse-monochrome image of the edge of the Sun, with jets of flame tens of thousands of miles high erupting from the surface – mosaic of photographs by solar photographer Gianluca Valentini

small, and sometimes politically unstable, regions. At the same time global population is rising and industrialisation around the world means that our global energy needs are increasing every day. Then, of course, comes the issue of pollution. Fossil fuels are unfavourable because they produce pollution, both of the smokes-and-smogs kind and also carbon dioxide, which contributes to climate change and on which subject much has been written. These are all serious problems telling us to wind down our use of fossil fuels now. It is clear that the world needs new ways to produce energy.

Now, we do have other energy options. Renewable energy sources such as wind, solar and hydro-power will help provide us with energy, but they have their own problems. One is that these sources are what's known as "low energy density", so one solar panel or one windmill doesn't produce much energy. You need a lot of them, and so they take up a lot of space. To replace one fusion power plant you'd need about a thousand wind turbines, each with a blade diameter of about 100 metres, so well over 300 feet. The other

A view inside the torus-shaped chamber of a fusion machine (called a tokamak) not in operation

The incredibly hot surface of the Sun with two sunspots in this shot by solar photographer Gianluca Valentini from 2007 June 9th. This picture is just under 64,000 kilometres or 40,000 miles in width: our Earth would only be slightly bigger than one of the sunspots

problem is intermittency, so when the sun doesn't shine or the wind doesn't blow there is no energy. We need to develop more efficient storage solutions, because at the moment electricity is very expensive to store. I'm not saying that we shouldn't use renewables at all - I think we need to use everything we can - but it's questionable whether renewables alone will be able to satisfy our rising energy demands.

If we were able to use fusion to generate electricity, it would go a long way towards solving all the world's energy problems. Fusion is the ideal energy source – it doesn't take up much space, it has an almost inexhaustible supply of fuels, it is safe, it produces no carbon dioxide and no long-lived radioactive waste.

The same tokamak interior when in operation – tiny amounts of plasma glow with intense heat

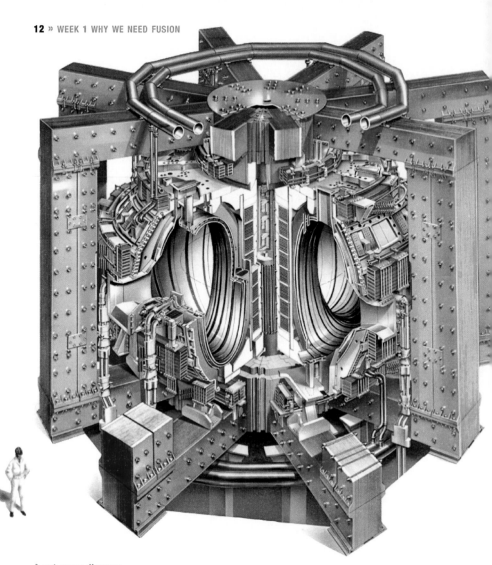

A cut-away diagram view of the European JET experiment, a fusion machine run by scientists from a consortium of countries, located in England's Midlands. Currently (2012), this experimental generator is the world's largest

In this book I'm going to tell you what fusion is, how we do it, and about the machines – called tokamaks – that we use. I'm also going to tell you about some of the physics behind fusion. Through this, you'll get an idea of how fusion works and how we hope to make the power stations of the future.

Next time we'll whizz through some basic atomic physics and the fusion reaction used in tokamaks, and I'll be visiting Liverpool.

Week 2   When Atoms Collide

The second destination on my country-wide lecture tour was Liverpool. I would be speaking at the University of Liverpool to pupils of various different schools in the area.

I drove up to Liverpool on Tuesday night. It was snowing for most of the way, but fortunately not settling. I stayed the night with a friend in Runcorn, just outside Liverpool. In the morning I drove into the city centre, to the University. I had borrowed a satnav, which made the navigating a bit easier and so I arrived quite early. I set up with plenty of time for a sandwich and a cup of tea before the talk.

Now, before we start to talk about the fusion reaction used in tokamaks, we're going to recap some basic atomic physics. In the talk I do this as a quiz to make it a bit more fun. It's not a very difficult quiz for GCSE students, because they should have already learnt all of this at school.

An atom consists of a nucleus at the centre and electrons that go round the outside, as in the illustration on this page. Back in 1897 when J.J. Thompson first discovered electrons, it was thought that the atom looked a bit like a plum pudding – a positive pudding with little negative electron-raisins embedded in it.

A very simplified model of the helium atom, with grapes for electrons going round the outside, apples for neutrons, and peaches for protons. Of course this is not to scale – electrons are much much tinier than this in reality – see page 14. There's nothing special about helium – all the chemical elements & isotopes are just made of atoms with different numbers of electrons, neutrons, and protons

Then Rutherford's students Geiger and Marsden did an experiment. They fired positively charged alpha particles at thin gold foil, about one atom thick, and detected how the alpha particles were deflected by the atomic nuclei in the foil. They found that while most passed through unaffected, some were slightly deflected and a few bounced straight back, which was unexpected and seemingly incredible. But from this they realised that the atom is actually mostly empty space with its positive charge and most of its mass concentrated at the centre. The model of the atom became more like that of the solar system, with a big, heavy nucleus at the centre and electrons orbiting around like planets around the Sun.

The nucleus is only 1/100,000th of the size of the atom. To get a feel for what this means, imagine standing in the centre of a large football stadium and holding a pin. If we scaled up an atom so that the nucleus was the size of the pinhead, then the tiny electrons would be moving around somewhere outside the back of the stands. Everything between the nucleus and the electrons would be just empty space. In fact, there is so much empty space in the atom that if you took out all the space from the atoms making up the human species we would all fit into a sugar cube.

In total there are around 100,000 alphabetical letters, digits, and other characters like / or ; in this book

The solar system model gets us a bit closer to the picture of the atom, but this cannot be quite right either, since circling like this the electrons would gradually lose energy and spiral into the nucleus. Atoms can only be explained by quantum theory, so we now think of an electron "cloud" surrounding the nucleus, where the electrons flit about, sometimes here, sometimes there, because in the quantum world particles can be in several places at once … .

However, strange and interesting as it is, I'm not going to go into quantum theory here. Instead, let's talk about the nucleus, since it is the nuclei that fuse. The nucleus is very small but contains 99.9% of the mass of the atom. It is made up of protons (positively charged) and neutrons (neutral, so neither + nor –) and so the nucleus has a net positive (+) charge.

The type of atom depends on the number of protons in the nucleus, for example hydrogen has one proton, helium has two, lithium has three. But the same type of atom does not always have the same number of neutrons, as this page's illustration shows. These three images all show hydrogen. All three have one proton, but deuterium and tritium have extra neutrons so are heavier versions of normal hydrogen, known as 'isotopes' of hydrogen. These isotopes of hydrogen are what we fuse in the tokamak.

In a neutral atom the positive charge of the protons is exactly balanced by the negative charge of an equal number of (equally but negatively charged) electrons. If the atom is missing one or more electrons then it is charged and is called an ion.

So now we come to the fusion reaction in tokamaks. Fusion is the combining of two smaller nuclei into a larger one. For fusion energy from tokamaks, deuterium and tritium will be combined to form helium and a neutron, see the illustration overleaf on page 16. This is not the same as the fusion reaction that occurs in our Sun.

In the Sun, fusion of hydrogen to helium happens in three stages: two protons combine to form deuterium (one emits a positron and turns into a neutron); the deuterium combines with another proton to form helium-3 (an isotope of helium with only one neutron); two helium-3 nuclei combine to form helium-4.

Fusion in the Sun proceeds very slowly, taking hundreds of million years for two protons to fuse. This

The nuclei of three isotopes of hydrogen: 1 is normal hydrogen with just one proton and no neutrons (sometimes called protium); 2 is deuterium, a heavier kind of hydrogen with two particles in the nucleus (hence the "deu"), one proton and one neutron; 3 is tritium, an even heavier type of hydrogen with three particles in the nucleus (hence the "tri"), one proton and two neutrons

is pretty lucky for us, since otherwise all the fuel in the Sun would have burned out before life on Earth could evolve, but it's not too useful a reaction for us to use on Earth to make energy.

Fusing two protons into deuterium is the slowest step of the reaction, so starting with deuterium saves time, as now protons and neutrons only need to be rearranged rather than turned into other things. There are a few different fusion reactions involving deuterium, but the deuterium-tritium (DT) reaction is considered the best for a power plant because it requires the lowest amount of energy to get it started and is the fastest.

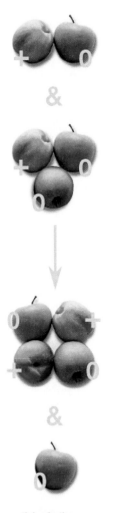

deuterium + tritium → helium + neutron

So that's the basic fusion reaction. After our discussion of atoms, nuclei and charges you may have picked up on a small difficulty in getting fusion to occur. We are fusing nuclei together, and the nuclei are both positively charged, so they will repel each other. Opposites attract, or like charges repel. They don't want to come together and fuse. Next time, I'm going to tell you how we overcome this force of repulsion and get fusion to happen.

How the particles in the two nuclei rearrange when deuterium fuses with tritium

Week 3 Cold Fusion / Hot Fusion

I had a busy week or so, with lots of talking in this section. I started off at the Big Bang Fair in Manchester last week, promoting science with the NOISEmakers and using some of my demonstrations to surprise the students and tell them some physics. This week I have been in the North West, mostly doing two talks per venue, so my voice is looking forward to a well-earned rest!

I spent the weekend in the Lake District and got out for a few nice walks. On Sunday I walked up to Stickle Tarn with an eighty-year-old National Trust volunteer who took some measurements at the dam. He was chatty and interesting, and often lamented that he couldn't speed up the hill "with his hands in his pockets" like he used to.

On Tuesday I went to Keswick, to a school with beautiful views who gave me big audiences of enthusiastic but well-behaved GCSE students. Lancaster on Wednesday was much quieter as the venue was the university and several schools dropped out at the last minute. The Burnley venue was interesting (but a bit stressful) to get to as the postcode was not recognised by the satnav and Google Maps sent me somewhere completely different! The pupils were quite shy about volunteering for demonstrations and asking questions. The two talks at Manchester MET were completely full and there was lots of interest, which was a nice way to finish the week.

So, you might remember from last ti
reaction we use in fusion machines (

deuterium + tritium → helium +

but that the nuclei are both positively
will repel each other. I said that this ti
you how we overcome the force of re

Well, we have to get the deuterium and tritium really hot. If something has a high temperature it means that the particles inside are moving very fast, and if our deuterium and tritium particles are moving fast there is more chance that they will slam into each other really hard and get close enough to fuse. We heat the fuel to 100 million degrees. That's 100 million Celsius, which is hotter than the centre of the Sun. At this temperature the deuterium and tritium gas becomes a plasma. Plasma is a charged gas, or the fourth state of matter. Let's consider each of these states separately.

The atoms in a solid are all very close together and have fixed positions. They have a little bit of energy, so they vibrate, but their shape together is fixed.

Give the solid some energy – heat it – and the atoms will begin to move faster. They will break away from their fixed positions and spread out a bit. The solid becomes a liquid. The atoms still have some attraction to each other so they will stay together and flow, and they will take the shape of the bottom of their container.

Heat it some more and the atoms will have even more energy and are even more spaced out. They move so fast that they can escape the attractions of other atoms, so escape from the surface of the liquid and

Plasma filaments in a low-pressure gas conduct electricity from the centre of the ball to the outside and illuminate a neon light tube – see page 20

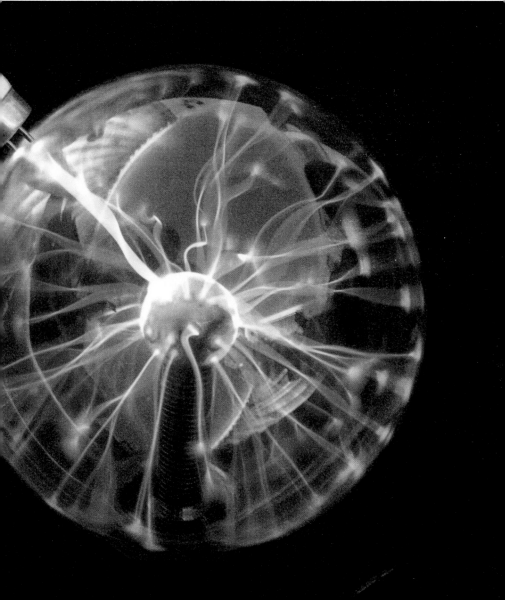

Pupils at some of the talks making and seeing plasma form inside the glass ball

move around wherever they like, taking up the whole container, or room, or whatever space they have. They become a gas.

Now if you heat it even more, and give the atoms even more energy, then the electrons have enough energy to escape from the atom. The electrons are stripped away from the atomic nucleus, and we have a plasma. We call this process *ionisation*. You can see in the diagram on pages 22 and 23 that plasma looks much like the gas except that there are two different types of particle moving around on their own. Instead of being full atoms, the electrons and the nuclei move around separately. Since these particles are charged we can say that a plasma is a charged – or ionised – gas, and a plasma can conduct electricity because the charges can move.

A plasma ball shows visually the plasma conducting electricity. The glass ball contains gas at low pressure, which makes it easier to ionise, or strip the electrons. Electricity flows into the centre of the ball and the only way for it to travel through the ball is to make a plasma. It has to strip away some electrons to carry the current. So the high voltage from the centre of the ball to the outside drives current to flow between the centre and the glass, and the path is shown by the coloured streamers. But the current does not flow through the glass, and this causes charge to build up at the glass surface, which generates an electric field. The electric field (along with the electric field generated at the centre of the ball) will induce current in nearby conductors, like the fluorescent tube shown here. The fluorescent tube is filled with gas and, again, the only way for the current to flow is for the gas to become a plasma to conduct the electricity.

A high voltage ionising air so that a current jumps across the gap generating a plasma. This is sometimes called a Jacob's Ladder apparatus

You may not realise it, but plasmas are all around us - you'll be quite familiar with some already, for example neon lights, the Sun, flames, plasma TVs, lightning …. The three photographs on these pages, 20 & 21, demonstrate making plasma with a high voltage – this looks like a cross between lightning and flames. Here, the high voltage across the small gap at the bottom of the 'V' shape ionizes the air so that the current can flow.

So that's a bit about plasma – charged gas that can conduct electricity. Not all plasmas are hot. That plasma ball, for example, is not at 100 million degrees. To make a plasma you just need enough energy to strip away some electrons. Low temperature plasmas are used in many industrial applications, from jet engine turbine blades to computer chips. But it's important to remember that for nuclear fusion the plasma has to be very hot indeed – more than 100 million degrees – so that the deuterium and tritium nuclei are moving fast enough to overcome the repulsion between them and get close enough to fuse.

Something you might have been wondering about while we were discussing the high temperatures fusion needs is "cold fusion". Cold fusion caused a storm in 1989 when two reputable scientists, Pons and Fleischmann, announced they had achieved fusion reactions in a test tube at room temperature. There was great excitement because it seemed so much easier to achieve than hot fusion.

In solids the atoms are orderly and close together - in fact helium is rarely a solid, and then usually its atoms are arrayed in the classic 'orange-crate packing'

In liquids the atoms are usually almost as close together, but they lose order

Gases expand to fill 3D space, and their atoms roam at long distances from each other

Pons and Fleischmann used the method of *electrolysis*
in a cell containing heavy water (where deuterium
takes the place of normal hydrogen) and electrodes
of the metal palladium. They attempted to force
deuterium created at the palladium cathode into the
metal to such high concentrations that the deuterium
particles would get close enough to fuse.

Unfortunately the research didn't stand up to intense
scrutiny from other physicists (what we scientists
call *peer review*) and so far there is no evidence that
what Pons and Fleischmann reported was actually
fusion, though some groups still continue cold fusion
research. In the absence of definitive proof, the fusion
research community will continue to pursue fusion
by heating the fuels to extremely high temperatures

In plasmas the atoms are not really
atoms any longer. Nuclei stay intact but
their electrons are stripped away so
that electrons and nuclei roam around
separately, and at even bigger distances
from each other usually than in gases

since the laws of physics tell us that to overcome the repulsive force between positively charged nuclei we need very fast-moving nuclei and therefore very high temperatures.

Now all this talk about plasmas that are hotter than the Sun surely prompts a pertinent question – how do we contain something that is hotter than the core of our own star? I'll be answering this question next time, when I tour from Gloucester to Truro.

More details about cold fusion can be found in Chapter 8 of Fusion: The Energy of the Universe by McCracken & Stott

Time off in the Lake
District around
Langdale

Week 4 Magnetic Fields

This past week I have been in the South West, and I have travelled all the way from Gloucester to Truro, in the South West of England. The weather for most of the week has been beautiful and I have driven through miles of glorious English countryside, green and shining in the sunshine. A friend put me up in the charming town of Truro, and this leg of the trip also let me stay in tiny villages with pretty stone cottages. There was an especially memorable old manor house bed & breakfast and a house with the River Piddle flowing through the garden.

Typically, whenever I had a day off, it threatened rain, so I put off my visit to the Eden Project but managed to squeeze in a coastal walk around Lizard Point before the showers began. The coast was beautiful and blustery. Strands of hair whipped around my face but my jacket kept the worst of the wind off, and striding out over the undulating cliff path kept me quite warm. When we dropped lower I caught that unmistakable smell of the sea, like oysters – salty and clean. Lizard Point is the most southerly part of the British Isles. Tourists sat drinking tea in The Most Southerly Café or looking out for Cornish choughs – a protected black cliff-nesting bird. As the clouds came in I dashed back along the path to my car, leaving the Lizard in the pouring rain.

So, back to fusion, and this week I'm addressing the question: how do we contain something that is hotter than the Sun?

Lizard Point, the southernmost point of Cornwall and England

Well, we can use magnetic fields. We said last time that plasma is a charged gas, and it is this effect that is very important for building fusion reactors, because charged particles can be controlled by magnetic fields.

Without a magnetic field, the charged plasma particles are able to move around wherever they like. But impose a magnetic field and the charges gyrate around the magnetic field lines.

This is simply circular motion, just as if you have a conker or horse chestnut on a string that you're swinging around. Here, the tension force on the string keeps the conker going round in a circle. The conker wants to fly off in a straight line, but the force along the string pulls the conker round incrementally so it travels in a circle. This is exactly what happens to a charged particle in a magnetic field. The charged particle is like the conker, and when it moves it feels a force, just as if it were attached by a string to the magnetic field line. So the charged particles are trapped circling around the field lines, and this is how we use magnetic fields to trap a gas that is hotter than the Sun!

Magnetic fields can be powerful. To give you an idea of how powerful they can be, you can do your own little demonstration at home. You need two tubes – one plastic, one copper (or some other metal that is not magnetic) – and 2 strong magnets (rare earth or neodymium). Have a race dropping the magnets down the tubes.

The magnet dropped down the plastic tube will win the race. This is because it just falls under gravity, so falls very fast. The magnet travelling down the copper tube goes a lot slower. Look down the tube and you'll see the magnet falling in slow motion – it looks more like it's floating to the bottom.

This effect is due to something called electromagnetic induction, which was discovered by Michael Faraday around 1830. Electric fields and magnetic fields are intimately connected – moving charged particles (currents) generate magnetic fields and changing magnetic fields generate currents. A changing magnetic field across a conductor causes an electromotive force, or a voltage, to be set up across the conductor, which motivates the free electrons in the metal to move and causes

The humble conker threaded onto a piece of string is a surprisingly good model for how a charged particle is held swinging in loops in the right kind of magnetic field (like a satellite held orbiting in a gravitational field)

Early spring in the
West Country

a current. So in our metal tube, the falling magnet creates a changing magnetic field, which generates eddy currents flowing in the tube.

Now, earlier we were talking about how charged particles moving in a magnetic field feel a force. Current is a flow of charged particles (electrons)

in a particular direction, so the current flowing in a magnetic field generates a force. The direction of this force obeys Lenz's law, which states that the force will act to oppose the change creating it. In other words, in the case of our tube and magnet, the falling magnet generates eddy currents, which themselves generate a force pushing back up on the magnet and slowing its fall.

Pupils at St Peters School York dropping magnets down the two types of tube to see for themselves the power of magnetic fields

Two tubes with identical diameters & lengths show the power of magnetic fields when you drop a magnet down each tube. The magnet drops down the plastic tube much quicker, because the magnet induces eddy currents inside the metal tube which slow the magnet down as it falls

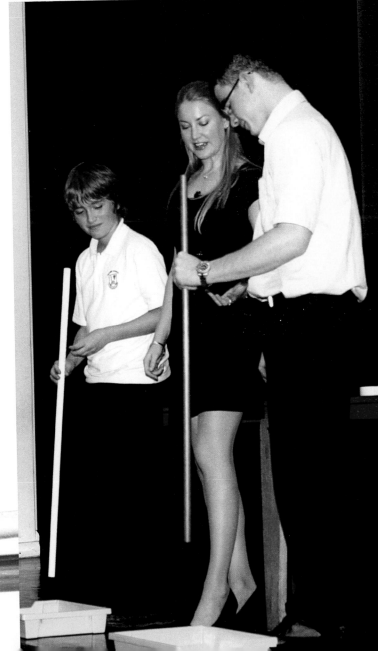

More falling-magnet races down plastic versus metal tubes

This brief foray into the delights of electromagnetic induction shows how charges and magnetic fields affect each other. It shows how we can use magnetic fields to trap the charged particles of a plasma that is hotter than the centre of the Sun.

Next time we're going to explore this containment in more detail. We'll be talking about *tokamaks* – the magnetic-trap machines that we use for fusion research – and I'll be speaking in Brighton and at the Royal Institution.

Week 5   Magnetic Bottles

The last couple of weeks the weather has been amazing, and I drove down to Brighton on a balmy Sunday evening. I drove past Brighton Pier, all lit up and twinkling, and in my hotel I was kept up half the night by squawking seagulls!

The school where I was speaking was in Rottingdean, just down the road from Brighton. The children were shy to volunteer, but more forthcoming and questioning in smaller groups after the talk. Since it was so sunny, I had my lunch on the beach and had a bit of a paddle before heading back to London.

тороидальная
камера с
магнитными
катушками

The lectures at the Royal Institution were great! Both audiences were really enthusiastic and fun to talk to. They asked so many questions they had to be stopped because we had run over time. It was so exciting to be speaking in such a famous and traditional venue - in the very building where Faraday made his discovery of electromagnetic induction.

тороидальная
камера с
аксиальным
магнитным
полем   .

Last time we were talking about how we can use magnetic fields to trap charged particles. There are a variety of machines that can be used to do this, such as the *tokamak*, the *stellerator* and the *reversed-field pinch*. The tokamak is the most successful and prevalent of the different devices, and it is a tokamak design that is currently the most likely candidate for a fusion power plant. So today I'm going to tell you a bit about the basics of tokamaks.

The two terms in Russian that give rise to the acronym 'tokamak'. This word is now used by fusion researchers worldwide to refer to a torus-shaped chamber holding hot plasma inside magnetic fields

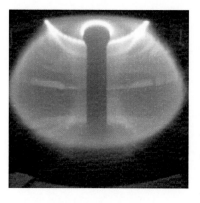

This is the first image in a short film from inside the MAST tokamak, showing the plasma when we stop the complex feedback system explained on page 35. When this stops and it is no longer controlled, the plasma moves, and once it hits the wall it extinguishes. This is called a disruption

Each frame is four 1/1000ths of a second apart. If you flick past the pages, you can watch the plasma move and disrupt

The two basic directions in a torus. 'Poloidal' means round the smaller circle, 'toroidal' means round the larger circle

Now you might be wondering where the word "tokamak" comes from. It's actually a Russian acronym. Tokamak stands for *toroidalnaya camera magnitsnaya katusha*. This means "toroidal chamber magnetic coils", which I rather like because it describes exactly what a tokamak is.

A torus is the mathematical name for a ring-doughnut shape. So a tokamak is a ring-doughnut-shaped (toroidal) vessel surrounded by magnetic coils that make the trap for the hot plasma and keep it from touching the walls.

Fusion experiments started as linear (straight line) machines, such as a solenoid, or a coil of wire, with magnetic field lines that went along its length. But while this trapped the charged particles along the field lines and stopped them escaping through the sides, particles could easily escape at the ends. The simple solution to this is to bend the cylinder round into a torus so the ends join up. This way the particles keep circling.

poloidal magnetic field

plasma ele
cu
(secon
transfo
ci

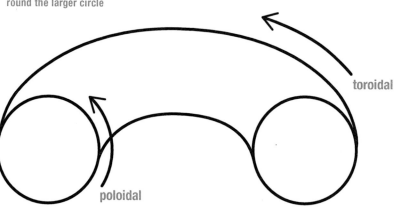

toroidal

poloidal

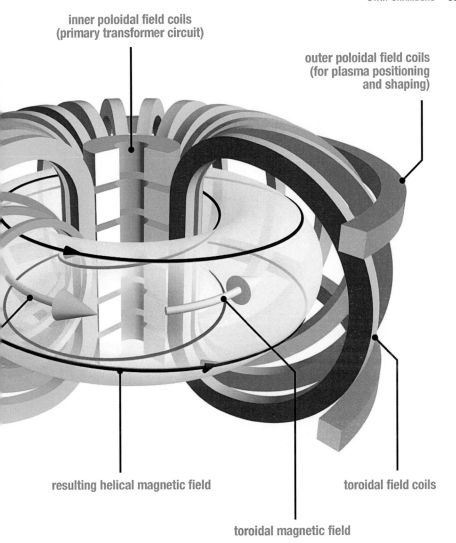

inner poloidal field coils
(primary transformer circuit)

outer poloidal field coils
(for plasma positioning
and shaping)

resulting helical magnetic field

toroidal field coils

toroidal magnetic field

Before we discuss the main features of tokamaks, it's useful to introduce some terminology. The main directions used in tokamaks are *toroidal* (the long way round the doughnut ring) and *poloidal* (the short way round) as shown in the simple diagram on the facing page.

The more detailed diagram above on this page shows the configuration of a typical tokamak. To make a magnetic field go toroidally around in the centre of

A coloured diagram showing the different magnetic coils inside a working tokamak, poloidal and toroidal fields working together to keep plasma clear of the inside walls

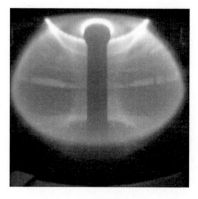

Frame from plasma disruption
film inside tokamak

Page 32 + 0.004 seconds

A set of profile
cross-sections from a
research tokamak in
Switzerland, showing
different shapes and
locations of plasma
inside one half of the
torus. The two larger
cross-sections in the
middle are the most
stable and central
plasma shapes and
sizes, enlarged for
emphasis, obtained
from http://crpp.epfl.
ch/tcv

TCV TOKAMAK
VARIOUS CONFIGURATIONS ACHIEVED

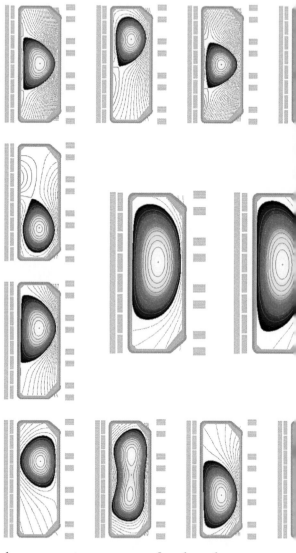

the torus requires a current to flow through magnetic
coils that encircle the vessel in the poloidal direction.
These are shown as the blue coils in the illustration
on page 33. It's the solenoid wrapped round on
itself, as discussed earlier. The magnetic field created
partially traps the plasma, but not very well. With only

a toroidal field the whole plasma will drift outwards gradually because of a special combination of the electric and magnetic fields acting on the charged particles.

The way to stop this drift is to induce a current flowing in the plasma in the same direction as the toroidal field (remember that plasmas can conduct electricity). This current then generates a magnetic field surrounding it in the poloidal direction, the green arrows in the page 33 diagram. The two magnetic fields in combination create a resultant magnetic field in a helical shape, the way the thread would go round a screw or bolt if you bent the bolt into a closed loop. The plasma particles spiral around the doughnut-shaped vessel and stay trapped. You can think of the toroidal field as trapping the plasma and the poloidal field as pulling the plasma away from the walls.

This is a simple explanation of what's going on, but building a tokamak is quite

Brighton – on a good day

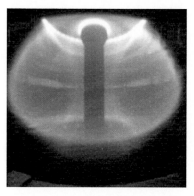

Frame from plasma disruption
film inside tokamak

Page 32 + 0.008 seconds

complicated. You have to get all the currents and magnetic fields right to hold the plasma in place, and even then it moves! The grey outer poloidal coils in the coloured tokamak diagram on page 33 are used to shape and move the plasma. Currents flowing in these coils will generate their own magnetic fields around them, which push against the magnetic field of the plasma because magnetic fields can't cross. These are used to keep the plasma stable and balanced. Complex feedback systems are designed to detect where the plasma moves and push it back into a central position. The poloidal field coils can also be used to make many different plasma shapes and some machines, like TCV in Switzerland, have many coils to do just that. The array of profiles in the diagram spread across pages 34 and 35 shows the various shapes TCV have achieved. The upright oblong frames with the top right and bottom right corners slightly truncated are vertical sections of one side of the torus. If the torus was like a perfect rubber ring, like the simple line sketch on page 32, those cross-sections would each be a perfect circle. The coloured blobs inside the oblongs are the plasma of course.

So that's a bit about tokamaks and how they trap hot plasma. Tokamaks come in many different shapes and sizes, all contributing to the overall fusion programme and being used for research all around the world. Have a look at the Tokamaks Top 10 at the end of this book to see some of the best. More than half the world is working together to make fusion happen.

Week 6   How To Heat Plasma

Another short week of lectures this week - just two. Tuesday saw me up very early and braving the M40 traffic to get into London for my talks in Camden. Then it was north into Hertfordshire for talks in Hatfield. Both venues had good audiences asking lots of questions. In Camden some of the students came out to the front afterwards to try some of the demonstrations - a chaotic ten minutes with sticky fingers on the plasma ball, neodymium magnets getting stuck together and variously-sized balls bouncing around!

In week 5, last week's chapter, we discussed the basic principles of tokamaks and this time I'm going to tell you a bit about how we heat the plasma to temperatures of around 100 million degrees.

There are three main forms of plasma heating: ohmic heating, neutral beam injection, and resonance heating.

You are already all familiar with ohmic heating. This is where conductors with a current running through them heat up due to their own resistance.

A good example of this is an old fashioned light bulb. The thin tungsten filament heats up so much that it gives off light. It gets hot because current-carrying electrons bump into atomic ions in the conductor as they move through, and during each collision energy is transferred to the ions. Temperature is a measure

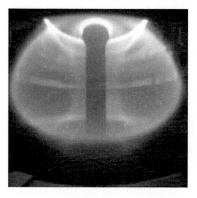

Frame from plasma disruption film inside tokamak

Page 32 + 0.012 seconds

of how fast the component particles are moving, so the more the ions get hit the hotter the conductor becomes.

In tokamaks, the current that is induced in the toroidal direction (flowing the long way around the ring, see the diagram at the bottom of page 32) heats the plasma by ohmic heating. However, this method is limited because as the plasma heats up to very high temperatures (millions of degrees) it becomes too good at conducting electricity and there is very little resistance to generate heat. After that, additional heating is required to increase the temperature to hundreds of millions of degrees. By targeting where the additional heating energy is deposited it can also be used to improve the plasma performance, meaning how well the turbulent plasma is trapped.

Neutral Beam Injection (NBI) is a way of heating the plasma by firing very fast particles into the plasma. Once inside, they crash into lots of the plasma particles and give up some of their energy, making the plasma hotter. The particles must have no net charge or they wouldn't get through the magnetic fields that trap the plasma (remember magnetic fields affect charged particles). You can think of NBI a bit like heating milk for a cappuccino. Steam is fired into the milk and it gets hot. Steam is high-energy water, and all the fast steam particles give up some of their energy to the milk.

Neutral beams with no net charge are usually atoms of hydrogen or deuterium. They have to be going very fast because they need enough energy to get them into the centre of the plasma and still have extra energy to give to the plasma particles. If they were going too slowly they would give up all their energy before they reached the centre. The atoms in the neutral beam used on JET, which is the biggest tokamak

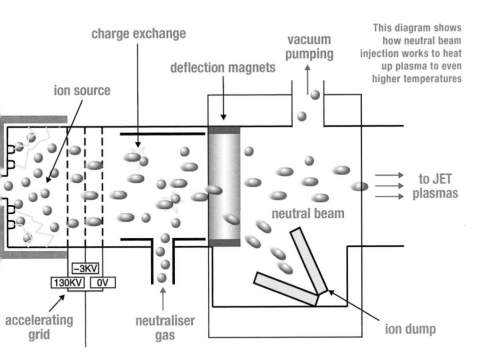

charge exchange

vacuum pumping

deflection magnets

This diagram shows how neutral beam injection works to heat up plasma to even higher temperatures

ion source

-3KV

130KV 0V

accelerating grid

neutraliser gas

neutral beam

to JET plasmas

ion dump

in the world, can travel at more than 3,000 km per second, which is well over six million mph. That's ten thousand times faster than the speed of sound.

Neutral beams are made by first taking charged particles (ions) and using an electric field to accelerate them to high speeds. At JET they use a voltage of more than 100,000V. The fast ions then pass through a neutral gas where some recombine to form neutral atoms that continue into the plasma. Any particles that remain charged are deflected by a magnetic field to an ion dump that absorbs their energy. The large diagram on this page shows the NBI system at JET.

The final method we use to heat the plasma is resonance heating. This uses electromagnetic waves,

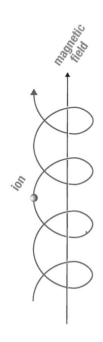

magnetic field

ion

An ion - the positively charged nucleus of an atom - moves in a helical path through a magnetic field

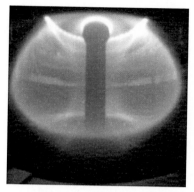

Frame from plasma disruption film inside tokamak

Page 32 + 0.016 seconds

La Sainte Union school

specifically radio waves. Many types of waves can travel though plasma. Depending on the local conditions in the plasma, sometimes they pass right through, sometimes they are reflected and sometimes they are absorbed. If they are absorbed, energy is transferred from the wave to the plasma particles, increasing their kinetic (movement) energy and heating them up.

We talked in Week 4 about how the magnetic fields trap the charged plasma particles – they gyrate around the magnetic field lines. They do this with a particular frequency (the number of circuits made per second) that is called the cyclotron frequency.

The heating is most efficient if the frequency of the wave (how many times it goes up and down in one second) resonates with the cyclotron frequency of the particles to be heated. In other words, the frequency of the radio wave must be the same as, or a multiple of, the cyclotron frequency. In JET the radio waves have a frequency of 23-57 MHz (FM radio frequencies are around 100 MHz).

So, heating will occur when the radio frequency and the cyclotron frequency resonate. The cyclotron frequency only depends on the particles' charge and mass and the magnetic field strength. The particles' charge and mass are constant, but the strength of the magnetic field decreases outwards across the torus, so the cyclotron frequency also changes across the torus. This means we can heat very specific regions in the plasma just by changing the frequency of the radio wave.

Next time we'll be talking about JET – one of the main world centres for fusion research. My next part of the tour takes me to Scotland in September, but I might try to write more before that, some time over the summer holidays.

Week 7 Building Test Chambers

Summer really seemed to fly by! It has been raining most of August and with all the wind this week it's been feeling quite autumnal, which can only mean one thing – the summer holidays are coming to an end and I'll soon be off on tour again. I did say I would write a bit about JET over the holidays, so here we go....

JET (the Joint European Torus) is the biggest tokamak in the world and the only operational experiment capable of producing fusion energy. As the name suggests, it is a European joint venture used by over 40 European labs and more than 350 scientists and engineers, under the European Fusion Development Agreement (EFDA). JET was built at the end of the 1970s on the site of a former airfield at Culham in Oxfordshire, England. Its construction took five years and it was happily completed on time and on budget. Its very first plasma was created in 1983 and it is still running today, 30 years later.

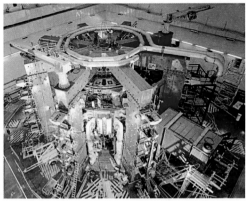

A view of the JET tokamak from outside the main chamber

In November 1991 JET achieved the world's first controlled release of fusion power. The Preliminary Tritium Experiment used 10% tritium in deuterium and produced power in the megawatt range. Then in 1993 the American tokamak TFTR (the Tokamak Fusion Test Reactor in Princeton) achieved fusion whilst operating with the 50-50 deuterium-tritium

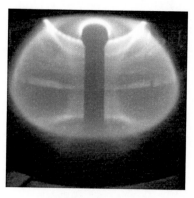

Frame from plasma disruption film inside tokamak

Page 32 + 0.02 seconds

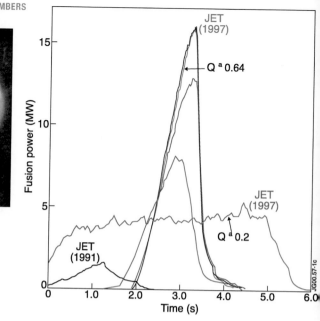

fuel mix of commercial reactors. The world record for fusion power was set in 1997 When JET produced 16MW, the graph immediate right shows the fusion power produced in the 1997 and 1991 experiments. In 1997 the power input was 24MW, so the power produced was only 65% of the power put in to create the fusion reactions, but it was still a massive achievement. JET has made real fusion reactions and

Inside the JET torus. A researcher checks the surface of the interior wall, which of course has to withstand immense temperatures during fusion tests

it hopes to get closer to break-even in the coming years after a big upgrade in 2011.

JET is a purely scientific experiment and has evolved over the years as the fusion field has progressed. It has been modified and upgraded frequently to answer new questions and test technologies for the next step fusion device – ITER. (ITER is currently under construction and will be a reactor-scale experiment that hopes to prove the technological feasibility of fusion power. I'll be telling you more about ITER next week.)

The photographs on pages 41 and 42 show the impressive size of JET. The machine is 18 metres high, 15m or 50 feet in diameter and the whole ensemble weighs thousands of tonnes[1]. In the centre, the doughnut-shaped vacuum vessel is about 8m across from the outside edges and holds a volume

The graph at the centre of the page shows how JET successfully spiked to an output of 16MW during an experiment lasting a few seconds in 1997. Although for a very short time, producing less power than the 24MW required to make the reaction happen, this was a major achievement and set a world record for fusion power out of an experimental reactor

Below is a simplified cut-away drawing of the tokamak coils

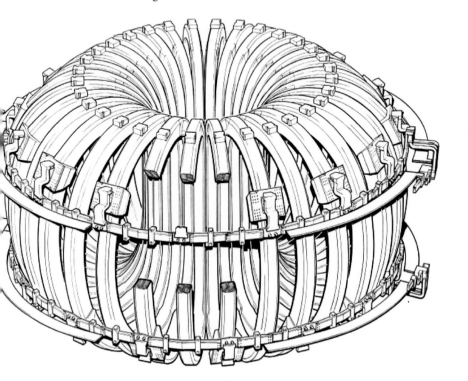

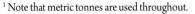
[1] Note that metric tonnes are used throughout.

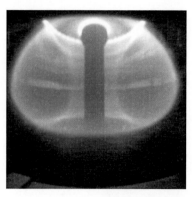

Frame from plasma disruption
film inside tokamak

Page 32 + 0.024 seconds

J.E.T. MECHANICAL STRUCTURE
EXTERNAL TO INTERNAL STRUCTURE FIXING DETAILS

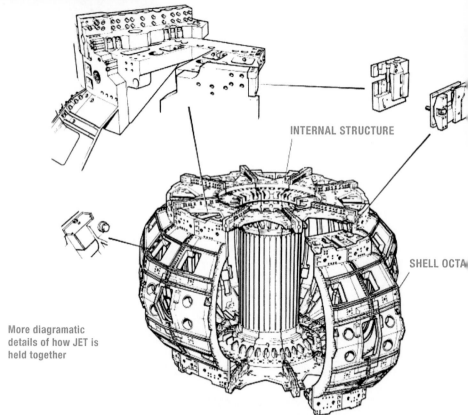

INTERNAL STRUCTURE

SHELL OCTA

More diagramatic
details of how JET is
held together

JOINT BETWEEN TORSION COLLAR AND RING

TORSION COLLAR

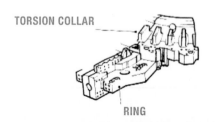

RING

JOINT BETWEEN TORSION COLLA AND INNER CYLINDER

INNER CYLINDER

TORSION COLLA

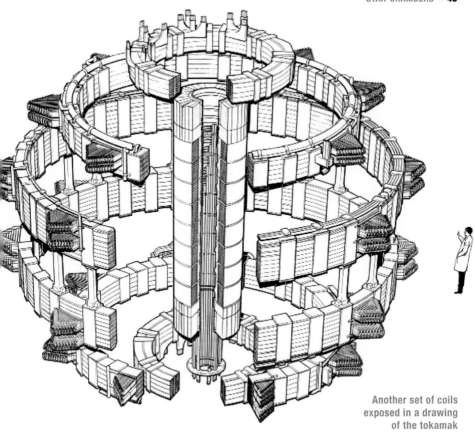

Another set of coils
exposed in a drawing
of the tokamak

of 80 cubic metres of gas, well over 2,000 cubic
feet. There are powerful auxiliary heating systems
(the Neutral Beam Injection and resonance heating
described last week), a pellet injector for refuelling (a
bit like a huge pea-shooter that fires tiny frozen pellets
of deuterium into the plasma) and a gas injector for
disruption studies (if the plasma is unstable and about
to hit the wall, pumping lots of impurity gas into the
vessel will smother the plasma and it will lose all its
heat and current very quickly).

JET also has about 100 diagnostic instruments for
looking at the plasma and taking measurements.
Scientists measure properties of the plasma like the
temperature, density, its position and how fast it is
rotating, and machine parameters like the strength of
the magnetic fields and currents flowing. There are

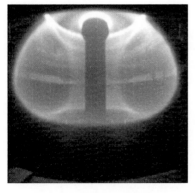

video cameras taking pictures in various parts of the spectrum, including X-ray, visible and infrared.

See pages 10 and 11 for a split photograph of the JET vacuum vessel. The left-hand half shows it empty. You can see the tiles on the wall and the gutter at the bottom, called the *divertor* (spelled with –or, not the usual –er) to which most of the heat and particles are directed by the magnetic fields. The right-hand half of the picture shows plasma in JET taken with a visible-light camera. You'll notice that it looks like there's not

Frame from plasma disruption film inside tokamak

Page 32 + 0.028 seconds

Fitting the pieces together to make the Joint European Torus

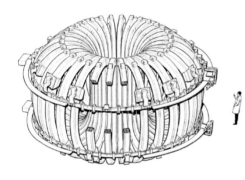

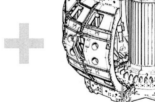

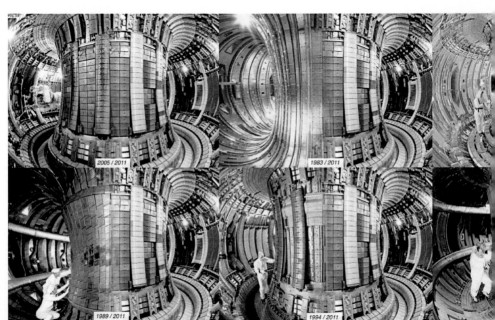

much there inside the toroidal vessel where we expect the fusion reactions to be taking place. But there is. Most of the plasma is away from the walls, but it's invisible. That's because it is so hot that the only light that the plasma emits (if it's emitting any at all, because light is only given off when electrons recombine with the nucleus of the atom and this is unlikely to happen much in the hot region) is X-rays or ultraviolet light. Only cooler things emit visible light, so we can only see the cooler parts of the plasma, which is at the edge, near the wall. The middle of the toroidal tube cross-

Regular maintenance work inside the JET tokamak chamber (photographs at bottom of page), with technicians removing and replacing tiles damaged by exposure to enormous temperatures during plasma fusion sessions

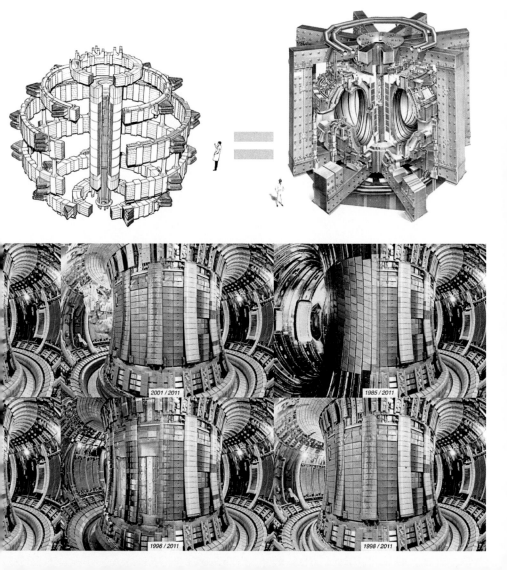

2001 / 2011

1985 / 2011

1996 / 2011

1998 / 2011

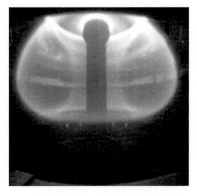

Frame from plasma disruption
film inside tokamak

Page 32 + 0.032 seconds

section is about 100 million degrees but the curved wall at the edge is only a few thousand degrees.

Follow this link to see a video of what a whole experimental plasma shot looks like in JET. http://www.melaniewindridge.com

In a couple of weeks I'll be travelling to Scotland and even doing an extra talk on the Isle of Mull, and in the next blog we'll be talking about the new fusion experiment, ITER, that is currently being built in France.

In the JET work hall
is a surrounding
superstructure. This
contains the torus.
It also provides
fuel, power to
the magnetic
coils, and holds
all the measuring
instruments. These
track what states
the plasma is in, as
well as what energy
goes in and out

Week 8 From JET To ITER

My fusion tour around Scotland took me to Glasgow, Edinburgh, Aberdeen and Inverness on consecutive days, so I've had busy days of talking and travel. There wasn't time to see much of the cities, but I did get to see lots of beautiful countryside in between and the weather wasn't nearly as bad as forecast. We drove down past Loch Ness (I didn't see Nessie) and past Ben Nevis (I didn't have time to climb it) and spent the weekend on the beautiful Isle of Mull, staying at Lip Na Cloiche – a lovely little bed & breakfast with an amazing garden and view over Loch Tuath. We went beachcombing for pretty and interesting objects and ate lots of seafood. On Monday we drove through the mist and rain to Tobermory, where I spoke at the

Scotland's Glen Nevis

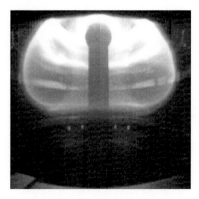

Frame from plasma disruption
film inside tokamak

Page 32 + 0.036 seconds

school, and on Tuesday we reluctantly took the early ferry back to the mainland and headed back home.

In the last fusion blog we were talking about JET, the biggest tokamak in the world. This week I'm going to tell you a bit about ITER, the next-step fusion machine that is even bigger than JET and is currently being built in France.

ITER is a worldwide collaboration of seven major parties – China, the European Union, India, Japan, Korea, Russia and the USA. It is a huge project that aims to prove the technical feasibility of fusion by getting ten times as much energy out of the fusion reactions as is put in to start them. It will also operate in similar conditions to those in a future fusion power plant and will test important reactor technologies such as helium extraction, tritium breeding and remote maintenance.

ITER is a huge machine that is about twice as big as JET and with ten times the plasma volume. It will be over 30 metres or over

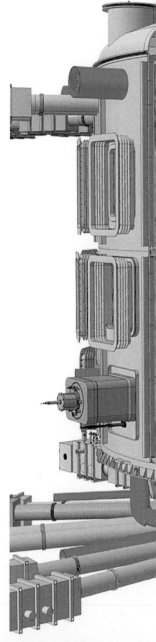

100 feet tall and will weigh 23,000 tonnes. Look at the diagram on this page and spot the man in the bottom right corner. The building to house it will stand 57m tall (that's almost as tall as a twenty storey building). 10,000 tonnes of magnets will control the plasma: 18

Just how much bigger ITER will be than JET should be clearer from this cut-away drawing

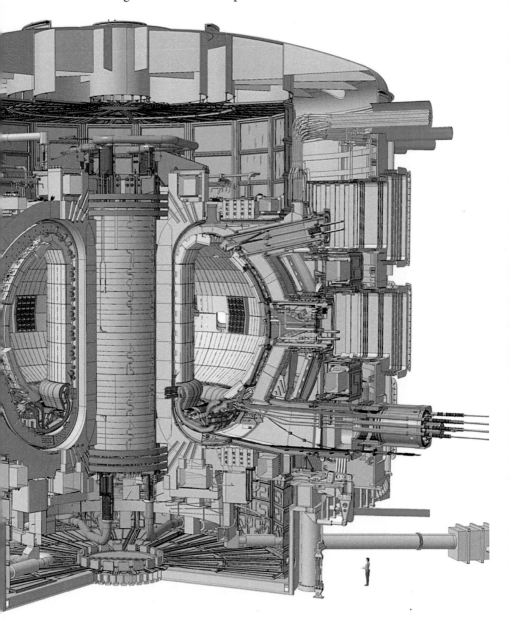

Frame from plasma disruption film inside tokamak

Page 32 + 0.04 seconds

The beautiful garden of Lip na Cloiche with a view out to Loch Tuath

magnetic coils to create the toroidal field that traps the charged plasma particles; 6 coils to create the poloidal field that pulls the plasma away from the walls and can shape and move the plasma. Visit http://www.iter.org/mach for an interactive diagram of the ITER tokamak to find out more about the different components of ITER.

The ITER vacuum vessel and magnets will sit inside a huge coolbox – the cryostat – that will cool the superconducting magnets using helium at -269°C. Superconducting magnets are needed for long or continuous operation. An experimental plasma shot in JET lasts only about 30 seconds and is limited by the copper magnetic coils. As currents flow through the copper coils to make the magnetic field the coils

heat up due to resistance. The coils are not allowed to get too hot, and they must also cool down again before the next shot can start. Superconductors are materials that have zero electrical resistance and so don't heat up, but the phenomenon of superconductivity only occurs in some materials below a certain, characteristic temperature near absolute zero.

Using superconductors for ITER means that the experimental shots will be able to run for much longer and that no energy will be wasted in the coils, so the power consumption will be next to nothing compared with JET's copper coils. However, the design of ITER will have to be a lot more complicated because of the cooling system for the superconductors. Superconducting coils are also much more expensive. The picture on this page shows the ITER magnets.

ITER was originally designed as an even larger machine back in the late 1980s to early 90s, but the project had to be delayed and scaled back to cut costs. In 2001 the newly-designed ITER was 75% of the size of the original design and budgeted at €5bn. Clearing of the site near Aix-en-Provence began in 2008 and construction has now started, but a combination of a number of factors (including redesigns and commodity price rises) means that the cost of ITER is now estimated to be €14bn.

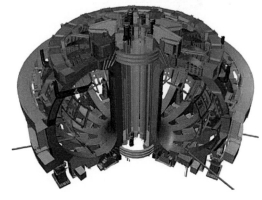

A cut-away drawing showing ITER's super-cooled magnets

Frame from plasma disruption film inside tokamak

Page 32 + 0.044 seconds

ITER is a costly project, but it is also major technological feat. Succeeding in fusion relies on the collaboration of scientists from many disciplines, such as materials science, engineering and plasma physics. It requires the development of sophisticated systems – for example vacuum and cooling systems – and advanced materials to withstand high temperatures and lots of fast, energetic neutrons. Fusion research and tokamak development pushes the boundaries of technology and stimulates innovation. Culham Centre for Fusion Energy promotes this and helps start-up companies using spin-off technology in areas such as magnetic resonance imaging, cheaper space travel by spaceplane and low-weight rechargeable batteries, to name just a few.

The roadmap to fusion sees the next-step fusion experiment, ITER, operating through the 2020s, demonstrating net power output and bringing together new technologies for reactor design. The 2030s should see a demonstration power plant (DEMO) produce electricity at the end of the decade, with commercial fusion plants to follow. This gets discussed further in Week 14.

Next week we'll be talking about robots being developed at JET – a technology essential to fusion reactor maintenance – and I'll be visiting Yorkshire and Derbyshire.

Week 9 Why We Need Robots

Saint Peter's School,
York

On my "fusion tour" last week I travelled between
York and Chapel-en-le-Frith, finishing in the heart
of the Peak District. The weather has been mostly
fine and, though I've been in schools during the
day, I've had some lovely evening drives through

Frame from plasma disruption film inside tokamak

Page 32 + 0.048 seconds

beautiful countryside. Thursday was particularly busy. A film crew from Physics World came to interview me and film some of the talk for a piece on their website as part of their special on nuclear power. I had a break on Friday and went for a long walk from Edale onto Kinder Scout. I have walked there before and the views are spectacular, but Friday was so misty that we could only see a few yards ahead. Large, eerie rocks loomed out of the fog and the wind was so strong on the plateau that my face burned and my hands were pulled back firmly into my sleeves. On Saturday I rushed into London for the Science Is Vital rally and by Sunday I was off again to Kent for another week of lectures ... but that's next week's story.

So in the last couple of sections I wrote about the biggest tokamaks in the world – JET in Oxfordshire and ITER, which is now being built in France. And this time I'm going to tell you about robots. Because JET has been pioneering robotic remote maintenance of tokamaks for several years now.

The reason we are going to need robotics in fusion power stations is radioactivity. Now I said in Week 1 that fusion doesn't produce any long-lived radioactive waste, and that's true. Fusion produces helium, which is safe. But the reaction also produces neutrons – very high-energy neutrons – that have no electric charge and so can escape the magnetic trap and fly out through the walls of the machine. And these neutrons have so much energy that that they can actually bash atoms out of place in the walls or induce nuclear reactions, changing the

material properties of the walls. This makes the structure of the machine slightly radioactive.

Now this is not long-lived radioactive waste like that which comes out of a fission reactor. It won't last for tens of thousands of years. After 50-100 years the radioactivity will have decayed away to a safe level and the materials could be recycled. But it does mean that humans will not be able to go inside the machine to make any repairs. So we will need robots. Or at least we will need, to be a bit more precise, semi-robotic prosthetic extensions that human technicians can operate at a distance.

The robots being used on JET look a bit like toy plastic snakes that some of us saw or played with when we were young. These snakes are made of many small joints, which give the extension great flexibility and enable it to enter through a small porthole and curve around the inside of the whole doughnut-shaped vessel to make repairs.

The snakey prosthetic itself is 10 metres, so a bit over 30 feet long and includes a manipulator section at the end that carries out all the work inside the vessel.

See the photograph of the robot arm across pages 58 and 59 with a section of the tokamak. The toolhead is remotely controlled from a control room a safe distance away, so maintaining the machine with a device like this is called "remote handling".

The remote handling system is a sophisticated set-up that includes

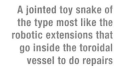
A jointed toy snake of the type most like the robotic extensions that go inside the toroidal vessel to do repairs

Frame from plasma disruption
film inside tokamak

Page 32 + 0.052 seconds

robotic devices, advanced computers, virtual reality
and closed circuit television, as well as specialist tools
required for repairs. Simulations are run before any
maintenance work is started then the procedures are
practised in a full-size mock-up of the tokamak. The
operator is given an experience like that of actually

being in the torus. CCTV gives a sense of sight and through the manipulator unit the operator has a sense of touch. Virtual reality gives accurate position perception. Visit http://www.melaniewindridge.co.uk/Star_Chambers.html to see a virtual reality animation of the JET robot.

A jointed extending arm fitted with tools, practising how it can snake around inside the doughnut-shaped chamber

Frame from plasma disruption
film inside tokamak

Page 32 + 0.056 seconds

Robotic prosthetics have been operating on JET since the early 1990s. The first complete divertor replacement by remote handling was made in 1998 and the robots are currently installing the new ITER-like wall for the new set of experiments beginning in 2011. Remote handling is an important technology to develop for the repair, maintenance and upgrade of future fusion power plants. There are additional benefits too. Using the robots gives increased precision and introduces fewer unwanted impurities into the vacuum vessel.

These robots – or prosthetics is really more accurate – are special tools which effectively extend the operator's own arms. They undertake a wide range of tasks like welding, cutting and bolting as well as inspection of the vessel. Often specific tools are specially developed at JET. The operators need to get a lot of practice in controlling the robots because the tasks being performed are very precise. They practice using a full-scale mock-up of JET and dummy components or, if they want to have a bit more fun, they can play giant Jenga. Have a look at this video on my website http://www.melaniewindridge.co.uk/Star_Chambers.html

Next week we'll be back on to another aspect of the fundamental science. I'll be writing about why fusion releases energy – and I'll be travelling around the South East.

Week 10 Where The Energy Comes From

Last week I started my lectures in Tonbridge, Kent, then moved north in a loop encompassing Milton Keynes, Peterborough and Woodbridge, near Ipswich, before returning home. In Kent I stayed in an oast house – a circular house with a conical roof traditionally used for drying hops for brewing. I didn't see much of the area because since the evenings have been drawing in I have been doing more and more driving in the dark (and sometimes the rain too). Unfortunately this week I saw more of the roadworks on the M25 than of the glorious English countryside, so I think the less said about that the better.

Tonbridge School

Frame from plasma disruption film inside tokamak

Page 32 + 0.06 seconds

Instead I'll move straight on to fusion. Last time the subject was the robotics used on JET, and this time we'll be talking about why fusion releases energy. This is to do with something called binding energy.

All nuclei have a binding energy, which says how tightly the nucleus is bound together. Energy is required to split a nucleus apart, so when a nucleus is created it releases this energy. Binding energy is really quite a confusing concept, but I like to think about it by likening the nucleus to an elastic band.

Take an elastic band and stretch it as far as you can – you have to put energy in to do that; you can feel it. Now let one side go and the elastic band will ping back to its smaller size, releasing energy. You can hear it – snap! This is what happens in the nucleus too. Splitting a nucleus apart requires energy – the binding energy – but when particles come together to make a new nucleus the reaction gives back all that energy.

Different nuclei have different amounts of binding energy. It's clear, then, that if we start with something with a lower binding energy and we make something with a higher binding energy we are going to release all that extra energy. The binding energy curve shows how binding energy varies with the size of the nucleus, and from this we can see why both nuclear fusion and nuclear fission release energy.

Any time we move upwards on this curve – when we go from a nucleus with a lower binding energy to one with a higher binding energy – energy is being released. In the case of nuclear fission (the splitting apart of heavy nuclei to make lighter ones) we start on the far right of the curve with a heavy nucleus such as uranium (marked

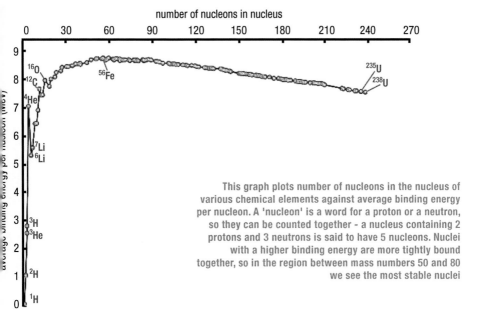

number of nucleons in nucleus

This graph plots number of nucleons in the nucleus of various chemical elements against average binding energy per nucleon. A 'nucleon' is a word for a proton or a neutron, so they can be counted together - a nucleus containing 2 protons and 3 neutrons is said to have 5 nucleons. Nuclei with a higher binding energy are more tightly bound together, so in the region between mass numbers 50 and 80 we see the most stable nuclei

^{235}U). This is split into two smaller fragments such as strontium (^{90}Sr) and xenon (^{143}Xe) about midway along the gentle downwards slope. You can see that we have moved up the curve from a nucleus with a lower binding energy to make two with higher binding energies, so that extra energy is what is released from the fission reaction.

In Week 2 of my tour we talked about the fusion reaction in tokamaks, which is

deuterium + tritium → helium + neutron.

Deuterium and tritium are isotopes of hydrogen – heavier hydrogen with extra neutrons in their nuclei. On the binding energy curve, deuterium is marked as ^{2}H, tritium as ^{3}H and helium as ^{4}He. At this side the curve is very steep so there is a big difference in binding energy between the ^{2}H and ^{3}H and the ^{4}He. Therefore, the fusion

A rubber band takes in energy when it stretches, and gives it back when you let go

Frame from plasma disruption film inside tokamak

Page 32 + 0.064 seconds

reaction, which makes ⁴He, releases a lot of energy, more even than the fission reaction.

Another way to think about why fusion releases energy is in terms of something called missing mass. It turns out that if you weigh the deuterium and the tritium that you start with, and then you weigh the helium and the neutron at the end, you find that the helium plus the neutron actually weigh *less*. During the fusion reaction some mass has been lost.

It was Einstein who said that energy and mass are equivalent and they can be transformed into one another. You've probably heard Einstein's famous formula $E = mc^2$ This says that the amount of energy released will be the change in mass times the speed of light squared. Light travels very fast – three hundred thousand km per second! So c squared is a very big number, which means you only need a tiny change in mass to release a lot of energy. This is why fusion releases so much.

You might remember that in Week 1, I said that just 1kg of fusion fuel releases as much energy as 10 million kg of fossil fuels – so ten million times as much energy. A very big multiple. That's because when fossil fuels burn it is chemical bonds that are being broken and when a nuclear reaction occurs it is nuclear bonds that are being broken. Nuclear bonds are much stronger than chemical bonds, so much more energy can be released, which is why nuclear reactions release so much energy.

To get an idea of the effect of multiplying by ten million, look at the first ever postage stamp, the Penny Black. Not even one square inch, each one measures ¾" x 7/8". If ten million Penny Blacks were laid end to end in a single strip, they would go round the M25 with still enough left over to get right into central London

Next time I'll talk about how we hope to convert the energy released by the fusion reaction into electricity, and I'll be travelling up to Newcastle.

Week 11   Which Atoms Do What

My visit to Newcastle was unfortunately short, especially considering how long it took me to get there. I was only there for one day, giving lectures at two different venues. The entire afternoon and evening of the day before was spent in the car – mostly in the dark, it seemed, because it was grey and rainy. Traffic was bad. My iPod ran out of batteries. I found a small café for a quick cup of tea and a flapjack and a friendly welcome, before I was back outside, running through the rain in the car park, diving into the car and joining the line of blurry red tail-lights again.

I arrived late at the small B&B in Hexham where I stayed the night. I awoke to a cold but clear, sunny day. From the breakfast room I looked out on a beautiful view across hazy countryside as I ate boiled eggs and toast. Allegedly the B&B was a small alpaca farm, but I didn't have a chance to look, I had to get to school. After the morning lecture I packed up my equipment and went into central Newcastle to the University of Northumbria. Trying to find the venue amid the fly-overs and junctions was interesting, but chance took me to the right place without too much trouble.

The afternoon lecture done I was back into the traffic heading south. I couldn't face driving the entire M1 on a Friday night, so I stopped off with friends in Leicester on the way back and completed the journey on Saturday morning. Sad my trip to Newcastle was so rushed. I didn't even see the Angel of the North.

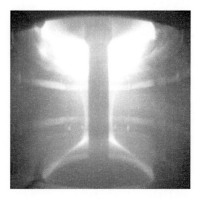

Frame from plasma disruption film inside tokamak

Page 32 + 0.068 seconds

In Week 10 we talked about why fusion releases energy. This time I'll tell you about how we get this energy out of the fusion reaction to make electricity.

You remember that the products of the tokamak fusion reaction are helium and a neutron. The neutron has no charge and can therefore escape the magnetic fields that trap the charged plasma, while the helium remains in the machine. The neutron also carries away most of the energy that is released. This is due to the conservation of momentum.

Momentum is the amount of motion that an object has and is defined as the mass of the object times its speed in a particular direction (momentum = mass x velocity). The more momentum an object has – so the heavier or the faster it is – the harder it is to stop.

When two things collide in isolation, the total momentum of the system stays the same – this is

1

2

Seeing how when two balls hit the floor together, the smaller ball bounces away much further, just like the neutron in the fusion diagram here carries away 4/5 of the momentum

80% energy

5 diagrams showing how deuterium and tritium approach, fuse, and then helium moves away with only 20% of the energy, but the single extra neutron moves off carrying 80% of the reaction energy, not unlike the smaller bouncing ball

20% energy

4

5

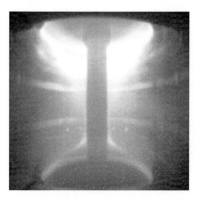

Frame from plasma disruption film inside tokamak

Page 32 + 0.072 seconds

the conservation of momentum. The objects in the collision will transfer momentum to each other, and what one loses the other gains, so both the objects experience equal and opposite momentum changes.

To get an idea of what happens you can do a simple demonstration yourself. All you will need are two balls of differing sizes. I use a basketball and a soft toy football, but you can use any. Just make sure that the smaller ball is not too hard (you don't want it to hurt if it hits anyone) and you've got enough space (it's probably better to go outside where the bouncing balls won't break anything).

First of all just drop – don't throw – the smaller ball to see how bouncy it is. Then stack the balls one on top of the other as I'm doing on page 6 7, and drop them together. If they bounce on top of each other you should see the small ball go flying off at speed – much more bouncy than when you dropped it on its own – and the big ball hardly bounces. This shows the small ball takes away most of the energy in this collision.

When the balls bounce, momentum is transferred from each ball to the other, but the big ball has more momentum and so transfers more to the small ball. It gives it a kick. The small, light ball then has a much bigger velocity in order to conserve momentum (momentum = mass x velocity).

So, just as the small ball takes away most of the energy of our collision, the small, light neutron takes away most of the energy of the fusion reaction. The neutron takes away four fifths of the energy released (14.1MeV) and the helium nucleus takes just one fifth (3.5MeV), as in the diagram across pages 66 and 6 7. And because the charge-less neutron can escape the magnetic trap, it flies straight out of the machine and we can use it. A fusion power station would use this neutron energy to make electricity.

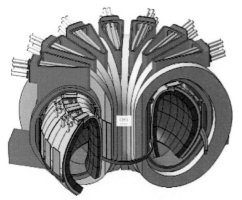

An overall view of the lithium blanket around the torus, left, made out of lots of wall modules

In a future power station, after the neutron passes through the first wall of the machine it will pass into a thick blanket, or layer, largely made of lithium enclosing the torus (doughnut shape), as in the drawing on this page top left. This simple diagram cuts through the torus, with the pink plasma in the centre and the grey blanket layer around the outside. The blanket will be made of lithium – the same material in your mobile phone batteries – and it performs two functions. Firstly, the lithium reacts with the neutron to form tritium, which is one of the fuels of the fusion reaction. Secondly, it heats up, and we can use that heat to make steam, drive turbines and make electricity just the same way that conventional power stations make electricity now. Let's look at the two processes separately.

Details of a possible wall module – the lithium blanket will be built out of lots of brick-like modules like this one below

Neutrons react with lithium to make tritium. There are two naturally occurring isotopes, or varieties, of lithium – ^{6}Li and ^{7}Li. Both reactions make tritium and helium; the reaction with ^{7}Li also releases a neutron.

$$^6Li + n \rightarrow {}^4He + T + 4.8MeV$$
$$^7Li + n \rightarrow {}^4He + T + n - 2.5MeV$$

The reaction with ^{6}Li occurs more easily, requires only a slow neutron to trigger it, and releases energy, while for the reaction with ^{7}Li to occur a fast neutron

Frame from plasma disruption
film inside tokamak

Page 32 + 0.076 seconds

is needed and the reaction absorbs energy. The issues associated with breeding the tritium fuel will be discussed in the next chapter.

The neutrons carry away 80% of the power of the fusion reaction. They pass easily through the first wall but are slowed down by collisions with atoms in the blanket, which heats up. At the same time, energy from the hot plasma heats up the first wall and a region at the bottom of the tokamak called the *divertor*, where the magnetic field channels lots of energetic particles. So the blanket, the first wall and the divertor will all heat up, and they will be cooled by high-pressure water or helium gas. This coolant will pass through a heat-exchanger and produce steam, which will drive the turbines to make electricity.

Lithium blanket designs will be tested in ITER during the later stages of the project, testing the heat-exchanging and tritium-breeding capabilities of different configurations. The blanket will be modular – made of many different pieces – to make maintenance and replacement easier. See the drawing on page 69 for a view of a wall module. In ITER it will be 440 individual segments, each measuring 1x1.5m and weighing up to 4.6 tons. But the ITER blanket will be made of high-strength copper and stainless steel – not lithium – and will act as neutron shield. Lithium blanket modules will be tested individually.

The lithium blanket is the means by which the energy of the fusion reaction is converted to electricity for our use. It is also a means of producing the tritium fuel for the fusion reaction. So while the fuels of the fusion reaction are deuterium and tritium, the actual fuels required for operation of a fusion power plant will be deuterium and lithium. The fuels will be discussed in more detail next time.

Week 12 Fuel Out Of Water

This week I've been to Bromsgrove in Worcestershire and Mansfield in Nottinghamshire. It was cold but sunny. One interesting thing I saw this week - leaning up against a wall in the old chapel at Bromsgrove School - is one of Scott's final Antarctic expedition sledges. It was quite a surprise. Apparently an Old Bromsgrovian, Reginald William Skelton, was an engineer and photographer on the earlier Discovery Expedition to Antarctica and the school also gave a sledging dog to the expedition.

Last time we spoke about how the energy of the fusion reaction converts into electricity by way of a blanket of lithium surrounding the torus. We mentioned how that lithium also reacts with the fusion neutrons to form tritium, one of the fuels for fusion reactions. This time we're going to talk more about the fuels a fusion power plant needs.

The fusion reaction that will be used for a fusion power plant is the reaction between deuterium and tritium, because it is the easiest to do, ie. it requires the lowest temperature. Remember that deuterium and tritium are heavy isotopes of hydrogen.

Deuterium is found naturally in water in concentrations of about 1 part in 6,700. This may not sound like a lot, but when all the water in the oceans

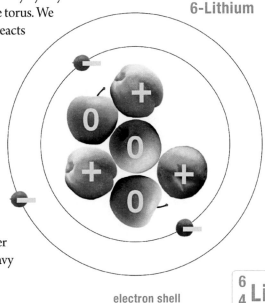

6-Lithium

electron shell configuration

$1s^2 \ 2s^1$

$^6_4$Li

Frame from plasma disruption film inside tokamak

Page 32 + 0.08 seconds

is considered there is about a million billion tonnes of deuterium, so a virtually inexhaustible supply. Deuterium can be extracted from water easily using electrolysis.

Tritium is radioactive with a half-life of 12.3 years, so it does not occur naturally on Earth. Small amounts of tritium are available as a by-product from some fission reactors, which can be used for experiments and for starting-up future fusion power stations, but for long-term fusion operation power stations will have to breed their own tritium fuel by reacting the fusion neutron with lithium. So the second fuel required for a fusion power station is really lithium.

Lithium is found in the Earth's crust in sufficient quantities to last for tens of thousand of years, but additional lithium could be extracted from seawater if necessary. Lithium exists in two natural forms, ^{6}Li and ^{7}Li, both with three protons and either three or four neutrons respectively. The reactions of the neutrons with these isotopes of lithium are:

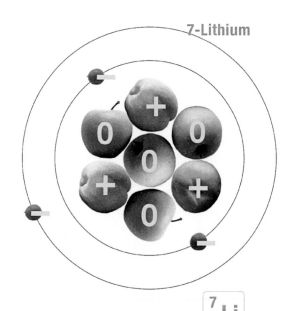

7-Lithium

electron shell configuration

$1s^2\ 2s^1$

$^7_4$Li

$$^6Li + n \rightarrow {}^4He + T + 4.8MeV$$

$$^7Li + n \rightarrow {}^4He + T + n - 2.5MeV$$

The important issue with tritium breeding is that since each deuterium-tritium reaction produces only one neutron, that one neutron must breed at least one tritium nucleus in order for the power plant to be self-sufficient. In tokamaks, not all of the plasma will be able to be completely surrounded by the breeder blanket, especially around the centre of the machine where space is tight. Also, some of the neutrons will be absorbed in the structure of the machine rather than reacting with the lithium, so the others will have to make more than one tritium nucleus to make up for these losses.

^7Li is important here because if a neutron reacts with ^7Li, then it produces not only tritium but also another neutron, which can then go on to react again. (The reaction with ^7Li requires energy of 2.5MeV to occur, but the neutrons

A photo opportunity next to Captain Scott's Antarctic expedition sledge

9-Beryllium

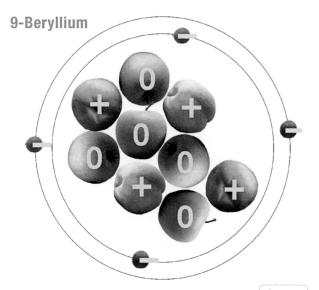

electron shell configuration

$$1s^2\ 2s^2$$

$$^9_4 Be$$

Frame from plasma disruption
film inside tokamak

Page 32 + 0.084 seconds

start out with 14.1 MeV so they have enough energy for this to happen).

Another way to increase the number of available neutrons is to introduce another material, such as beryllium, into the blanket to produce neutrons, which can then go on to react with lithium and produce tritium. Beryllium reacts with a neutron to form two helium nuclei and two neutrons:

$$^9Be + n \rightarrow {}^4He + {}^4He + 2n$$

When ITER is running, experiments will be done to test different designs of lithium blanket, including what chemical form the lithium should take (such as lithium/lead or lithium/tin alloys, lithium oxide or other mixtures) and whether or not a neutron multiplier such as beryllium will be needed. We think it might, but we're not sure yet. There are always new things to learn in science.

So we have seen that the fuels required for a future fusion power plant will be deuterium and lithium, both of which are abundant, spread evenly around the world and are relatively easy and cheap to extract. Moreover, because of the huge amount of energy that fusion produces, very little fuel will be needed compared to fossil-fuel power plants. The fuel costs for fusion will be very low indeed compared to the cost of constructing the fusion power plants.

Bromsgrove School

Week 13 Special Materials

This week my lecture tour took me to Didcot in Oxfordshire. It's an area I know well because Culham Centre for Fusion Energy is less than half an hour away. I worked there for four years. In winter, when the trees were bare, I could see the huge cooling towers of Didcot power station from my office at the lab. In the summer I spent a lot of time by the river, just a few minutes away from where I lived in Abingdon. One night in August I watched shooting stars (the Perseids meteor shower) whilst huddled under a blanket in the park. Many autumn hours were spent foraging for blackberries, apples, crab apples, sloes and even quinces – any freely-available wild fruit – and making jams, fruit crumbles and sloe gin.

Now it feels like we're well into winter and the last of the autumn picking has gone. It has been snowing this week in London and Buckinghamshire, so I was a bit worried about driving. However, as I moved north-west into Oxfordshire the snow became less and less. In Didcot there was no snow at all, just ice. I was freezing! Even in the car I had to wrap up in my woolly hat, scarf and gloves.

The lecture venue was the Rutherford Appleton Laboratory, home of the Diamond Light Source, the ISIS neutron source and the Vulcan laser. Here they do research into laser fusion as an alternative to using magnetic fields. It was at RAL that I got my first taste of plasma physics, doing work experience in solar-terrestrial physics during one summer holiday. I watched the launch of the Cluster mission spacecraft by live video link to the RAL lecture theatre – the same theatre that I was now lecturing in.

Frame from plasma disruption
film inside tokamak

Page 32 + 0.088 seconds

There are a number of challenges on the way to commercial fusion power. One of the most important steps is to show that we can get more energy out of the fusion reaction than we put in to get it going. This is fundamental if we want to build a power station!

Fusion scientists use a value called Q when assessing the energy balance. Q is the ratio of energy out to energy in, so $Q=1$ is breakeven and a Q of greater than 1 means that more energy is being created than consumed. Currently the world record is $Q=0.65$, held by JET for the production of 16MW of fusion power in 1997, as mentioned in Week 7. The Magnetic Confinement Fusion community hopes to better this record in the next few years. JET received a major upgrade in 2010 and with these improvements hopes to get closer to breakeven, or even exceed it, when the machine next operates with a real fusion fuel mix (deuterium-tritium) in 2015.

And then there is the new fusion machine currently being built that will be bigger and better than JET – ITER, see Week 8. ITER will be twice as big as JET in

A composite graph superimposing predicted and measured times a plasma remains confined from 13 different research tokamaks worldwide. Notice that ITER, now being built in France, is planned to set new record confinement times some distance outside any current times achieved

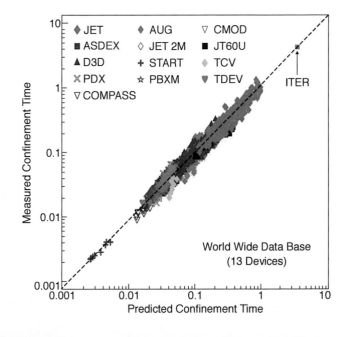

all dimensions with eight times the plasma volume. ITER hopes to achieve a Q of at least 10 – so that's ten times as much energy out as is put in – simply by virtue of being bigger. This is because something that is bigger stays hot for longer, and to make fusion power we have to be able to keep the plasma hot enough for long enough for fusion reactions to occur.

Heat makes its way out from the very hot plasma centre to the cooler edges by swirling, turbulent eddies, and the further this hot stuff has to travel to get to the edges the longer we'll be able to keep the plasma hot. The time it takes the heat to leave the plasma is called the *energy confinement time.* Detailed computer modelling of turbulence along with measurements of the energy confinement time for other, different-sized machines, allows us to predict the energy confinement time for a bigger machine like ITER and using this we can predict how much power we will get out.

Apart from achieving energy break-even, most of the challenges towards commercial fusion power

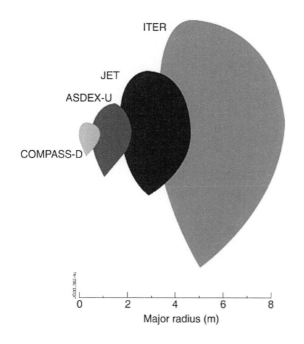

Comparing idealised sections of plasma cross-section inside different research tokamaks (ITER is still in construction – this shows its planned plasma profile). If a torus cut into the page and had its main axis in the plane of the page it would look like two circles or loops. These shapes are the plasma sections we would see inside the right-hand loop of each tokamak

Frame from plasma disruption film inside tokamak

Page 32 + 0.092 seconds

are now in engineering and materials science. We need to answer questions such as: How do you design a machine to hold a plasma hotter than the Sun? What materials do you use for the walls? How do we minimise radioactivity in the structure of the machine? We need to learn how to actually build a fusion power station.

Building a fusion power station is tricky because the fusion environment is a very hostile one – there are high temperatures, high pressures, high magnetic fields, high currents, very high-energy neutrons. These create conditions that are very bad for materials, so they will degrade more quickly. Yet someone building a power station who wants to make money will want it to operate for at least forty years without having to replace bits, so if fusion is to be commercially viable these challenges will have to be overcome.

Material scientists are working on developing new materials for nuclear power stations – materials that will be long-lasting, less prone to fractures and

A graph showing magnetic field lines around the plasma profile inside the JET torus

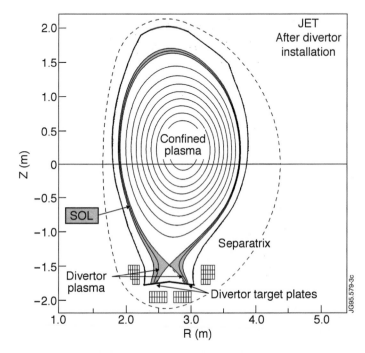

will become less radioactive over the lifetime of the machine. Neutronics experts study the damage caused by neutrons and how this affects the lifetime of materials and how radioactive they become. Also, engineers have to design machines that can withstand the harsh conditions, such as the tremendous pressures and forces created, as best they can. They also have to design machines so that if – as likely – parts of the tokamak have to be replaced periodically they can be replaced quickly, easily and cheaply without shutting down the power station too often.

ITER will study important aspects of fusion power plant design. It will test designs of lithium blankets to extract energy from the fusion reaction and breed more tritium fuel, as discussed in Week 12. It will check exhaust systems to get helium out of the plasma while the machine is running. It will test the suitability of particular materials for the inner wall of the central vacuum vessel – the wall closest to the hot plasma. Ideally, we want something that won't melt, will distribute heat quite evenly, won't easily get into

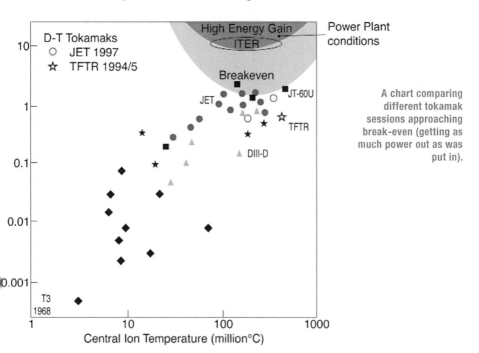

A chart comparing different tokamak sessions approaching break-even (getting as much power out as was put in).

Frame from plasma disruption
film inside tokamak

Page 32 + 0.096 seconds

the plasma contaminating it. But there isn't really one perfect material, so we will probably use different materials in different parts of the vessel depending on which property matters most in that area.

JET is currently testing wall materials that will be used in ITER. Beryllium has been chosen for the main part for the vacuum vessel because of its high melting point (1280°C) and small atomic size, which means that if it gets into the plasma it doesn't dilute the plasma as much as heavier elements.

Tungsten will be used for most of the divertor region of the vessel, where most of the plasma energy and particles are channelled if they reach the plasma edge. Tungsten has the highest melting point of any metal. A photograph (immediately right of this text) inside the JET vacuum vessel shows the divertor channel in the floor shot in normal light and, on the right side, in infra-red light. The divertor gutter around the base is the hottest part of the vessel.

The diagram on page 77 shows the pattern of magnetic field lines that the charged particles follow. In the central, concentric rings the particles are trapped, but any that escape into the yellow area follow the open field lines into the divertor. The points where the magnetic field lines hit the wall are the places in the machine that get the hottest and get the most particle bombardment, comparable to rocket nozzles. ITER will be using carbon fibre composite in these regions. This has high thermal conductivity, which means it can distribute the heat away easily, but it's not a good choice for use in the rest of the vessel because it readily combines with hydrogen and so can hold on to radioactive tritium.

Another consideration is that the machine must to be very strong to withstand forces that are created during an event called a disruption. Frames from a short film, just a few thousandths of a second, of one of the disruptions I researched, are in the top left-hand corners of the even pages from page 32 on. A disruption is when something causes the plasma to lose all its energy suddenly, like if we lose control of the plasma and it hits the wall. I have said before that the plasma is very turbulent. It moves. A tokamak uses sophisticated control systems to restrict this movement and keep the plasma in position.

Disruptions were my area of research and I studied them in the MAST tokamak at Culham Centre for Fusion Energy. Check those experimental pictures at the top of the even pages, 32 to 88. We want to keep the plasma nicely balanced in the centre of the vessel, but over just fractions of a second, something happens. The plasma moves up so high in the vessel that it hits the top. All the light you can see at the top of the picture is being emitted by the plasma as it cools down quickly and free electrons recombine with the ions (the atomic nuclei).

Disruptions are not dangerous – there is not a big explosion when the plasma hits the wall – because despite the very high temperature of the plasma there is so little stuff there (about the weight of a postage stamp in a machine as big as JET) that the plasma doesn't have enough energy to melt through the wall. Hitting the wall cools the plasma down very fast, leaving just some ordinary gas in the machine. But these disruptions do create large forces that cannot be ignored.

As the plasma moves, and when it hits the wall, electric currents are induced in the metal walls of the machine. In the presence of the strong magnetic fields used to trap the plasma, these currents generate forces.

Page centre: view inside a tokamak, with the photograph split between normal light (left) and infra-red (right), showing the hottest regions during a fusion session

Frame from plasma disruption film inside tokamak

Page 32 + 0.1 seconds

This phenomenon of electromagnetic induction was explained in Week 4, and if you did the demonstration with the tubes and magnets you would have seen what powerful forces are created when currents flow in magnetic fields – the force was strong enough to slow the falling magnet down considerably.

The higher the magnetic field and the current in the plasma when it hits the wall the larger the forces will be. In a large tokamak, the magnetic field and the currents that can flow into the walls are so high that the forces induced can be several hundred tonnes. The biggest (accidental!) disruption that ever occurred on JET caused the entire, huge machine to jump almost half an inch off the floor! Engineers design tokamaks to withstand disruptions like these, and at the same time physicists like me study them to get a better understanding of what is happening so that we can try and prevent them or minimise the damage they cause.

So we still face various challenges if we are going to make fusion a viable energy source, but we know much of what needs to be done. The problems aren't insurmountable. What is clear is that scientists from many different fields – plasma physicists, material scientists, neutronics experts, engineers and more – will all be working together to make fusion happen.

View from my office window. Coal-fired power station cooling towers only partly hidden by trees – a thing of the past if fusion can get past break-even point

Working out how to make a commercial fusion power station will take time, probably a few decades, so there is plenty of interesting work for young scientists and engineers coming into the field for years to come. We also need the machines and facilities to do this research. I'll be talking about this in the next chapter and visiting Wales.

Week 14 Making It Happen

After lecturing in Didcot I headed further west towards Wales, where I visited Swansea and Cardiff. On the way I stopped in Bristol, where I stayed with friends for the weekend.

I know Bristol well because I did my undergraduate physics degree at the university. Something I never did when I lived there was to visit the SS Great Britain – Brunel's famous iron-hulled steamship. She has an interesting history as a transatlantic passenger ship, an emigrant ship to Australia, a goods vessel and finally a coal bunker in the Falkland Islands before being deliberately sunk there in 1937. Over thirty years later she was recovered and sailed back to Bristol, where she now sits in the dry-dock where she was built.

Bristol had escaped the snow, but the pavements were treacherous with ice. On Sunday morning I went for a run round the Bristol docks and, perhaps foolishly, up the steep back-roads of Clifton. Going up was fine, and the view from the Royal York Crescent was lovely, but going back down was slippery and scary and I had to pick my way carefully.

On the Sunday afternoon I headed on to Swansea and, later in the week, to Cardiff. On Monday I had a free day in Swansea and I went for a lovely walk on the frosty Gower Peninsula to Three Cliffs Bay. On the cliffs, bracken and brambles were frozen rigid, leaves rimmed with ice and sprouting fragile crystals. Even the sand was frosty in places. As I drove back towards

Frame from plasma disruption
film inside tokamak

Page 32 + 0.104 seconds

London after the lectures the landscape was so white
it seemed the M4 snaked through Narnia.

Last time we talked about some of the major
challenges on the way to commercial fusion power.
Developing the technology required to build a fusion
power station is imperative, and crucial for this are
experimental machines and testing facilities.

ITER, the next-step tokamak, has been mentioned
several times and examined in detail in Week 8.
ITER will prove the scientific feasibility of fusion by
achieving $Q > 1$ (create more energy than it consumes)
and fusion power of 500MW, but it will also be
bringing together specific physics and engineering
capabilities on the scale of a power station for the first
time. Plasma physicists will be interested to see how
the bigger plasma behaves and whether or not the
plasma is more unstable at this scale. ITER will be a
feat of engineering – many of the engineering systems,
like the cryopumps and the exhaust systems, have
never been tested altogether in such a large machine.
But ITER is still primarily a scientific experiment. It

A cut-away view of IFMIF (image thanks to
IFMIF/EVEDA), the projected materials-testing
centre. IFMIF would enable special materials
to be tested over time in parallel with
next-generation tokamak technology. The
alternative is the new engineering lessons
being learned only one at a time, which is
much slower

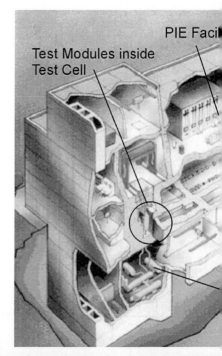

PIE Faci

Test Modules inside
Test Cell

will only produce about a third the amount of neutrons as a real reactor and will only operate for a few hours per day, so other testing facilities will be needed alongside ITER if we are to develop the technologies required for a power station.

A materials-testing facility will be essential to determine and test the best materials for the structure of the power station. The plan is to build the International Fusion Materials Irradiation Facility pictured at the bottom of this page, which will bombard materials with neutrons of a similar energy to those created by fusion reactions. IFMIF will use two particle accelerators to make beams of high-energy deuterons (deuterium nuclei) and fire them at a lithium target, stripping neutrons out of the deuterons. The neutron bombardment will be 24/7 for many years. IFMIF will not only test conventional materials that are in use now, but will also help develop advanced and improved materials.

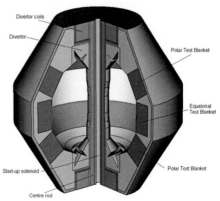

A depiction of the proposed Component Test Facility

DEMO – still bigger than ITER – would be the true prototype test power station, and would be aiming to multiply the input power 25 times

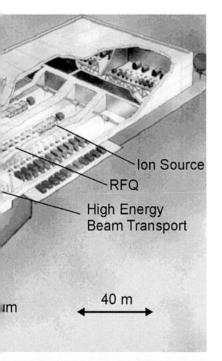

Ion Source

RFQ

High Energy Beam Transport

40 m

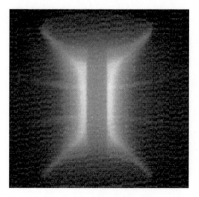

Frame from plasma disruption
film inside tokamak

Page 32 + 0.108 seconds

As well as testing materials, whole components of the future fusion power stations must also be tested for their durability over long periods of time to high-energy neutrons and high temperatures. For example, pieces of the wall and the surrounding blanket (Week 11) should be tested in fusion-reactor conditions for several years to ensure they can withstand the hostile conditions. Currently the systems that convert neutron power to electrical power are purely conceptual and have never been tested at all. Ideally, a Component Test Facility (CTF) should be built to do this – something small and affordable (~€1bn) – maybe based on a tokamak like MAST that is more squashed up and spherical than an ordinary tokamak – see the cut-away drawing on page 85, top right. There are currently no firm plans to build one, but it is vital these tests get carried out before a demonstration power plant is built.

How the timetable
(thanks to EFDA-JET)
might work out for
developing fusion
projects in the near
future - at least if we
get it right

The planned demonstration power plant will be called DEMO (see the projected design on page 85, lower right). This will be the machine that brings together all that we learn from ITER, IFMIF and CTF to put electricity onto the grid. It will be the final step before real, commercial fusion power stations are built. DEMO will probably be similar in design to ITER, but bigger, and hopes to achieve Q=25 (25 times as much energy out as put in). It will be of a similar scale to modern fossil-fuel-driven electric power

Year	0		10	
ITER	Construct			Operate
IF MIF	Design	Construct		Operate
DEMO	Explore	Concept	R&D	Design

plants. If everything goes to plan, DEMO should be in operation by the mid-2030s.

A spectacular view of Gower Peninsula

So these are the machines that we are going to have to build before we can make a real fusion power station. But now you're probably wondering when we think that will be. When will mankind first be able to start using fusion power? This is a difficult

30

onstruct   Power production

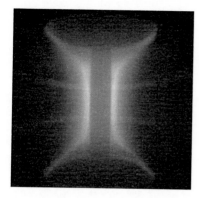

Frame from plasma disruption
film inside tokamak

Page 32 + 0.112 seconds

Frozen brambles during
one of the chillier
walks

question because it depends on many factors – not least political will, funding and good scientists and engineers coming and bringing new ideas to the field. It is currently believed that an orderly, properly funded, fusion programme could lead to fusion power in the late 2040s to early 2050s, assuming that there are no major surprises with ITER.

It may be possible to achieve fusion power sooner, but this will mean taking more financial risks. Constructing the machines described here so that they run at the same time, rather than one after the other, would mean we learn the required lessons earlier and could progress more quickly. Ideally the Component Test Facility should be built in parallel with ITER and IFMIF. We could also build an earlier DEMO. It would be a lower-performance model than could be built after all the experiments on ITER, but we would learn valuable lessons in engineering and power station construction that could then be fed into building a new and improved DEMO after ITER.

In the previous chapter I described some of the hurdles yet to be overcome if the world is to benefit from fusion power. In this chapter I have described some of the machines that we are going to build to find out the answers to our questions and overcome those hurdles. Fusion is not an easy target, but it is a very exciting one. Success is not guaranteed. But it is clear that the world needs fusion, and if we can overcome these tremendous scientific and technical challenges, fusion will give us clean, safe and abundant energy in the future.

The Rival to Tokamaks   Lasers

In this book we've taken a journey to learn about fusion. From why we *need* fusion through the fusion reaction and hot plasmas, to the machines that we use to trap these plasmas – the tokamaks. But this is just one way of doing fusion. We call it *Magnetic Confinement Fusion* because we are using magnetic fields to trap our hot fuel. But there is another way – using lasers.

The most important things for fusion are heat, pressure and confinement; we need to trap the fuel and keep it hot and dense enough for long enough for fusion to occur. We've talked about how tokamaks use magnetic fields to contain and pressurise the fuel (Weeks 4 and 5), and how we heat it using Neutral Beam Injection and resonance heating (Week 6). We can also confine and heat the fuel using lasers. This method is called *Inertial Confinement Fusion* but is more commonly known as *laser fusion*.

For laser fusion, the deuterium and tritium is contained in a tiny spherical pellet smaller than a peppercorn. This is blasted from all sides by hundreds of high-power laser beams approximately a million million times more powerful than a standard light bulb. These lasers deliver their energy in pulses that are a billionth of a second in length. The lasers blow off the outer surface of the pellet, which compresses the inner fuel down to such extreme temperatures and densities that it's like making a miniature star on Earth. The fuel is compressed to about one thousand times solid density so that all the atoms are very close together. Then shockwaves forming as the fuel compresses travel through the pellet and stop in the centre of the dense fuel, heating it to more than 100 million degrees – ten times hotter than the Sun. At this temperature the nuclei can fuse.

These are the four stages in laser fusion.
1. Fuel pellet blasted on all sides with high-power laser beams.
2. Outer surface of pellet blows off, compressing the fuel within.
3. Shock waves travel through the fuel and stop in the centre, heating it.
4. Fusion occurs at the centre and energy carried by the helium nuclei heats the rest of the fuel so that the fusion "burn" propagates outwards.

Between these two methods of creating fusion energy there are, in fact, many similarities. All of the general fusion science is the same. The fusion reaction and the fuels are the same; both methods have to overcome the electrostatic repulsion between the nuclei to get them to fuse; both will extract the fusion energy and generate electricity in a similar way. All this applies to fusion in general and not the particular method we use. So in this book, Weeks 1 to 3 and 10 to 12 apply to both magnetic and laser fusion, while the rest are specific to creating fusion using magnetic fields in tokamaks. As described, the main differences between magnetic and laser fusion are how the fuel is contained and how it is heated.

Research into the two methods progresses in tandem. It is hard to predict which will be the first to achieve commercial fusion power. There are significant challenges on both sides. In the case of Magnetic Confinement Fusion, these are outlined in Weeks 13 and 14. Of course the first problem is getting more energy out of the fusion reaction than is put in to start it.

Whereas in laser fusion, some of the main challenges involve ballistics, debris and the lasers themselves. Essentially it involves firing a tiny, frozen fuel pellet into the exact centre of a vast spherical chamber, and hitting it with around 200 laser beams at the same time. Accuracy is paramount. Beam lines are aligned at the pellet to a fraction of a hair's breadth; mirrors must be exquisitely polished and positioned on the microscale; the energy of the lasers must be distributed symmetrically over the pellet, which also must be kept frozen until hit by the lasers.

Heat from lasers causes the surface of a pellet to explode inwards, or implode. (Image adapted from a General Atomics graphic) This happens with enough force to raise the centre of the pellet to incredibly high temperatures, high enough for fusion to occur

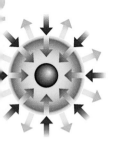

In this kind of environment, debris is not merely an inconvenience. It is a menace. When the pellet is hit by the laser some of it fuses and burns up, but the rest is splattered all over the target chamber. This debris contaminates the vacuum and could damage the laser optics, such as degrading the reflectivity of the mirrors that direct the laser beams. The extent of debris-induced damage still needs to be tested, but current thinking in reactor design is to reduce the exposure of optics to debris through careful positioning.

Then the lasers themselves provide challenges. Currently, the lasers we need for power stations don't exist. We have high-energy lasers that need hours to recharge or

low-energy lasers that can fire many times per second. We need high-energy lasers that can fire over and over again very quickly. Currently the high-energy ones can only fire a few times a day – we need them firing four times per second. Development work is going on in this area, and advances will have other applications besides fusion. These new types of laser will hopefully be available in the next 5 to 10 years.

Other challenges are similar to those faced by magnetic confinement fusion. Materials science and neutronics are very important for both because

Technicians descend into the super-clean target chamber to do maintenance. Notice the portholes for laser beams and diagnostics

ooth methods produce high-energy neutrons that will degrade materials. So the materials-testing facility, IFMIF, will be essential for the laser fusion community too. There is also the problem of instabilities in the plasma, which can cause the pellet to not compress symmetrically and then not get hot enough for fusion.

In the UK, much laser fusion research is performed at the Central Laser Facility at the Rutherford Appleton Laboratory, home to the Vulcan Petawatt laser. The largest and most energetic laser in the world is the *National Ignition Facility* at the Lawrence Livermore National Laboratory in California, USA. NIF uses 192 giant lasers to focus more than 1 million joules of laser energy on the tiny pellet. The lasers are aligned to the accuracy of a diameter of a human hair and the ten-storey building the lasers are housed in is as big as three football pitches. Look at the picture at the end of this section just to get an idea of the size of these facilities.

Some time in the next year or so, NIF hopes to get more energy out of the fusion reaction than it takes to run the laser, so the lasers may pass the breakeven Q=1 level (breakeven) before the tokamaks. We have to wait and see. The photograph on this page shows technicians on a lift in the NIF target chamber, surrounded by portholes for laser beams and diagnostics. The tiny pellet will be positioned in the centre of this chamber and the lasers focused onto it, as shown in the simplified diagram below right.

A simplified diagram showing laser beams being simultaneously focused on a pellet

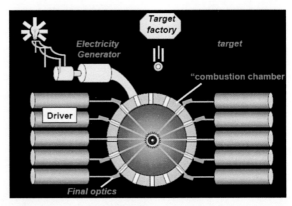

The next step for the laser fusion community will be the High Power laser Energy Research facility (HiPER). This is a European project that plans to test the viability of laser fusion as an energy source and will act as the next step towards a commercial fusion reactor. Across Europe, researchers are working on engineering, pellets and laser design, and HiPER will join together all the parts of this jigsaw in the next decade or so. The illustration is an artist's impression of what HiPER will look like.

Future fusion power stations will be similar regardless of whether they use magnetic fields or lasers. Since the main difference is how the fuel is heated and contained only the central part of the power station will vary. Outside the core similar principles will be used: lithium in a surrounding blanket will react with neutrons to form tritium; heat exchangers will transform the energy of the fusion reaction to electricity.

So laser and magnetic confinement fusion experiments complement each other. Scientists can share knowledge in areas like materials science, neutronics, basic plasma physics and diagnostics[1]. The experiments are also used to increase our knowledge in other areas, including laboratory astrophysics, extreme materials science and medical physics.

Whichever way we do fusion in the future, the machines – particularly the first generation – will be of impressive size. They will be true feats of engineering. There are challenges, but we hope that human ingenuity will surmount them. Humans have developed flight, put men on the moon using less computing power than found in today's average mobile phone, built skyscrapers hundreds of storeys high …. Cracking fusion will bring obvious energy benefits to mankind, but we will also learn a lot more along the way. Our research to overcome the fusion challenges and to build these huge machines will both push forward the boundaries of knowledge.

The large building needed to house HiPER (image thanks to HiPER)

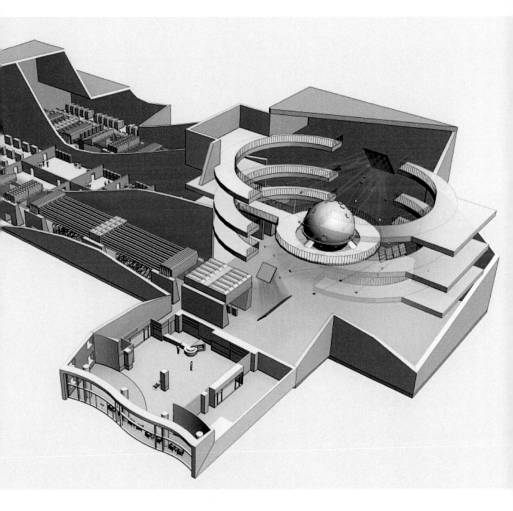

[1] Diagnostics are apparatus used to measure plasma properties such as temperature and density. They include equipment like spectrometers, interferometers and cameras among others.

With an impressive combination of size and precision, the National Ignition Facility, NIF, at the Livermore Labs in California USA, leads world laser fusion work at the moment

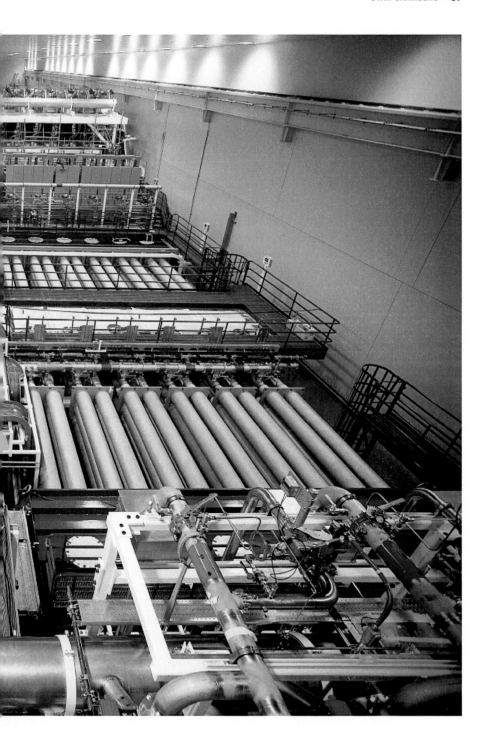

Tokamaks Top Ten

Over 200 tokamaks have been built around the world in the past 60 years of fusion research and almost 50 are still operating today. There are many different designs so that the experiments can study plasmas and fusion in different conditions. There are also two classes of tokamak: conventional (doughnut-shaped) tokamaks like JET; and spherical tokamaks, which are squashed-up and shaped more like cored apples than doughnuts.

This is my Top 10 of the largest, currently-operating tokamaks, based roughly on tokamak size and interesting features.

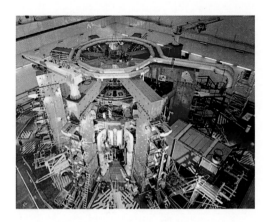

JET – Culham, UK – world-leading European tokamak holding world record for fusion power produced, 16.1 MW. Upgraded in 2010 to an ITER-like wall, testing beryllium, tungsten and carbon composite. Also the only device with remote-handling equipment and capable of using tritium.

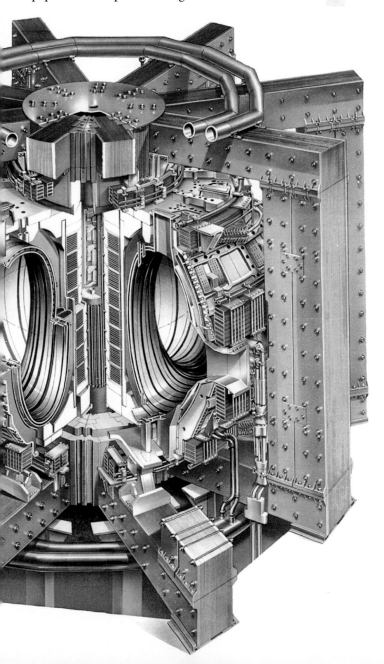

JT-60U – Naka, Japan – large tokamak with a plasma volume similar to JET. JT-60U holds the record for fusion triple product (density x temperature x confinement time) with an equivalent Q value of 1.25, which would pass break-even if the machine could use tritium.

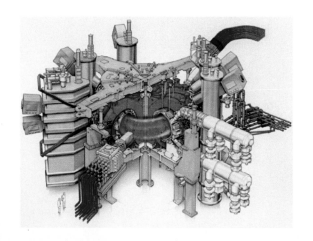

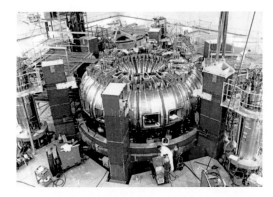

Tore Supra – Cadarache, France – holds a plasma with circular cross-section and has superconducting magnetic coils and an actively-cooled first wall so it can achieve long pulses several minutes long.

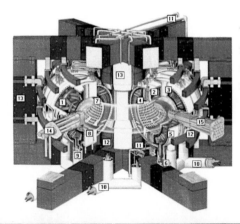

The world's largest superconducting tokamak researching steady-state operation. Longest pulse length of 6 minutes[1].

[1] The record for pulse duration is held by the retired tokamak TRIAM-1M, which was in operation in Japan between 1986 and 2005. TRIAM-1M's longest pulse lasted 5 hours 16 minutes, although at low power.

DIII-D – San Diego, USA – the largest operating tokamak in the USA, it has 18 shaping coils allowing for plasma shapes ranging from circular to triangular.

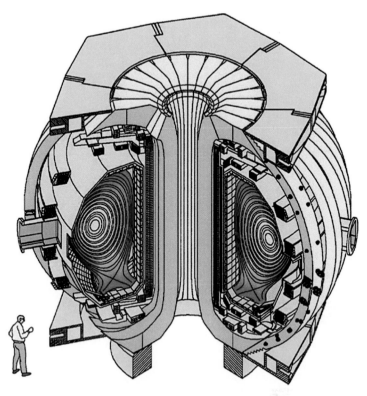

Asdex-U – Garching, Germany – the third-largest fusion device in Europe, this tokamak has full tungsten walls and high heating power.

Asdex
Upgrade

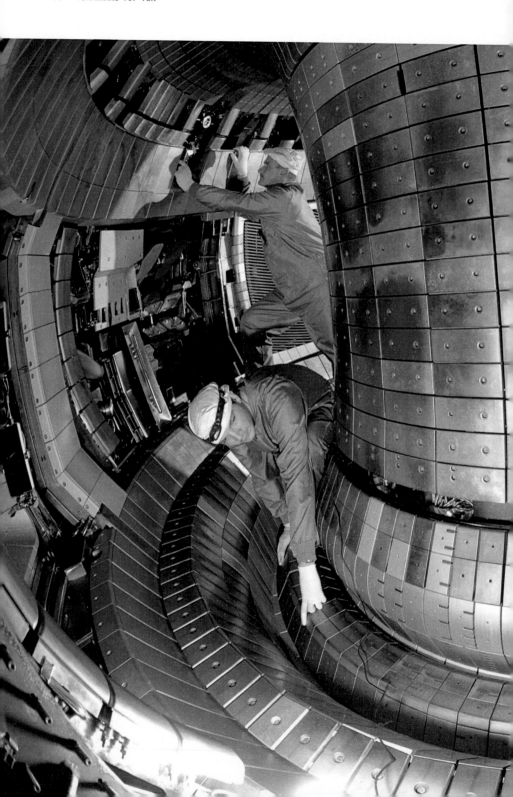

6

MAST – Culham, UK – "spherical tokamak" design with interesting open vacuum vessel design with magnetic shaping coils on the inside allows for full-plasma pictures. MAST is undergoing a major upgrade to get longer pulses and more heating power, and to test future reactor systems.

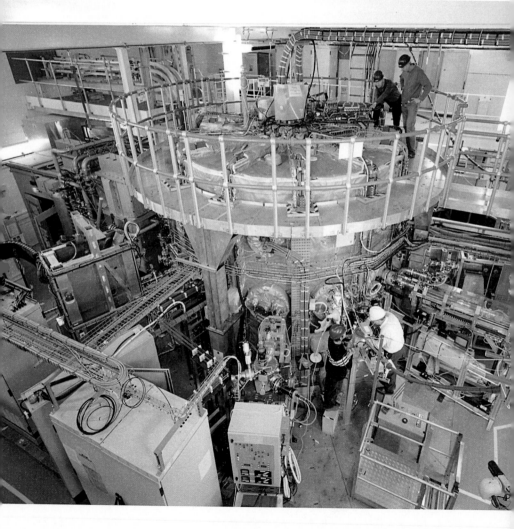

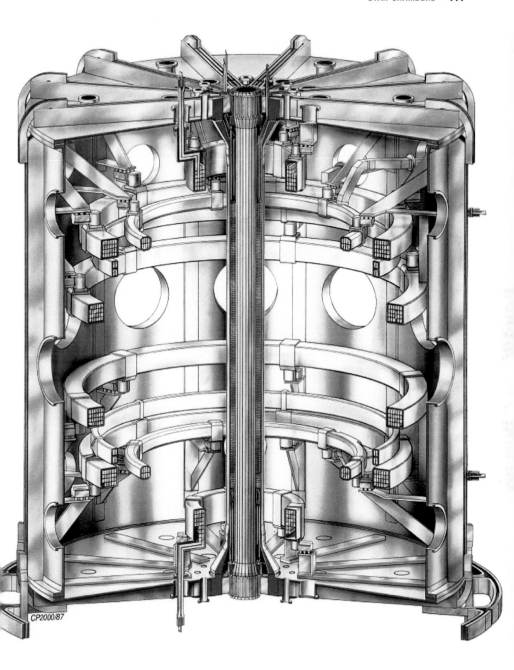

CP2000/87

KSTAR – Deajeon, South Korea – with superconducting magnetic coils and shaping coils KSTAR hopes to get pulses over 300 seconds long (5 mins).

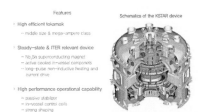

Features

› High efficient tokamak
    – middle size & mega-ampere class

› Steady–state & ITER relevant device
    – Nb₃Sn superconducting magnet
    – active cooled in-vessel components
    – long-pulse non-inductive heating and current drive

› High performance operational capability
    – passive stabilizer
    – in-vessel control coils
    – strong shaping

Schematics of the KSTAR device

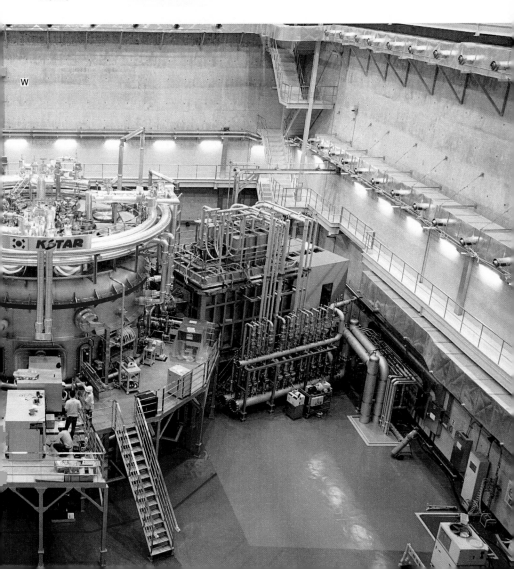

NSTX – Princeton, USA – spherical tokamak design like MAST but with a close-fitting wall. Holds the record for a quantity called β that relates to the economics of fusion power production.

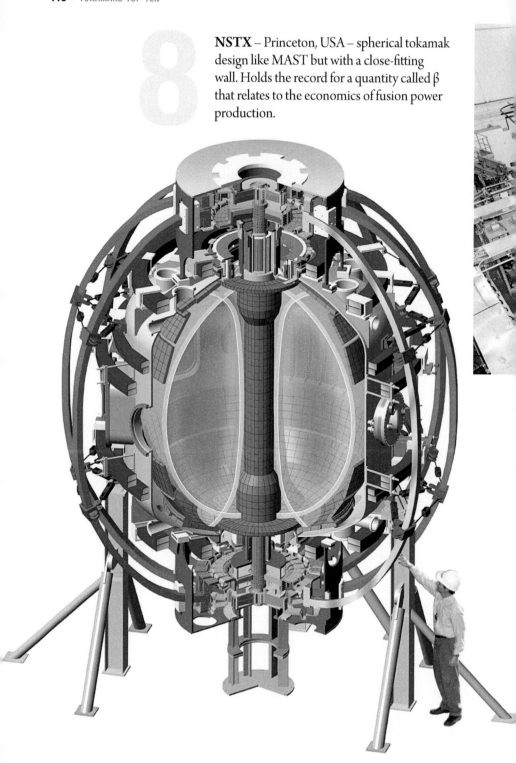

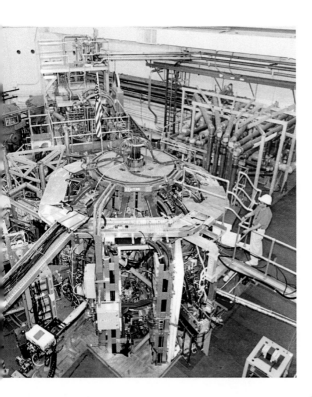

TCV – Lausanne, Switzerland – has 16 shaping coils that allow for very variable plasma shapes. Holds the record for the most elongated plasma cross-section in a conventional tokamak[1].

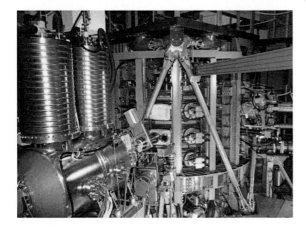

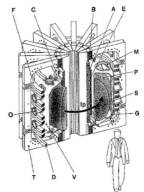

[1] It is easier to make an elongated plasma in a spherical tokamak than a conventional tokamak because the plasma is naturally more squashed up. Elongated plasmas generally give better performance.

10

EAST – Hefei, China – the first fully-superconducting machine with a non-circular (elongated) plasma cross-section.

This tokamak is designed for pulses up to 1,000 seconds.

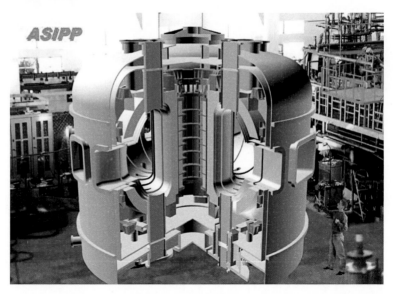

Technical information and pictures for most of the tokamaks built since the 1950s can be found on Nick Balshaw's tokamaks website at http://www.tokamak.info.

Acknowledgements

Firstly, to the Institute of Physics, particularly Clare Mills and Charles Tracy, for organising the IOP 2010 Schools and Colleges lecture tour that started all this.

To colleagues at Culham Centre for Fusion Energy for their support during the tour and the writing process, for fact-checking and for providing images not only of experiments but of a more general nature.

To Imperial College for continuing to host me as an academic visitor, for support, advice and interesting discussions.

To the Ogden Trust for their support in getting the fusion talk out to other schools after the IOP tour.

Significant Dates

Francis William Aston develops the mass spectrometer for precise measurement of atomic weight and discovers a large number or isotopes (varieties of the same chemical element with different masses)

Discovery of the atomic nucleus by Ernest Rutherford

1911

1919

905

1920   »

Revolutionary paper by Albert Einstein states the equivalence between mass and energy: $E=mc^2$

Arthur Eddington solves the problem of what powers the Sun - fusion. Using Aston's precise atomic weights and Einstein's equivalence principle Eddington shows that the mass difference between four hydrogens and one helium provides enough energy to power the Sun. It was realised that fusion was the mechanism but no-one really understood the process

To Garry McCracken for talking to me about fusion history and answering general questions.

To Nick Balshaw at www.tokamak.info for information for the Tokamak Top 10.

To Kate Lancaster and others at the STFC Rutherford Appleton Laboratory for advice on the laser fusion chapter.

To Sabina Griffith at ITER for all her speedy efficient help.

To David Morris at St. Peter's School, York, for the pictures of demonstrations in the lectures.

The editor wishes to thank Barbara Zachar for help checking Russian and Gianluca Valentini for the use of his solar photographs.

Significant Dates

The name "plasma" for an ionised gas is coined by Irving Langmuir, because it carries special particles like fast electrons and ions, rather like blood plasma carries red and white corpuscles

The first deuterium-deuterium fusion reactions are observed in the Cavendish Laboratory, Cambridge, by Oliphant, Harteck and Rutherford. The reaction creating tritium and helium-3 was also identified theoretically, though these wouldn't be observed until later

1927

1934

1932

James Chadwick discovers the neutron

To all the labs that kindly provided fusion images:

JET	EFDA-JET
JT-60	JAEA
Tore Supra	CEA
DIII-D	General Atomics
ASDEX Upgrade	Max Planck Institute for Plasma Physics
MAST	CCFE
KSTAR	National Fusion Research Institute
NSTX	Princeton Plasma Physics Laboratory
TCV	CRPP-EPFL
EAST	ASIPP
NIF	Lawrence Livermore National Laboratory
IFMIF	Lab F4E
HiPER	Rutherford Appleton Laboratory
CRPP-EPFL	Centre de Recherches en Physique des Plasmas

Thank you.

The UK and the USA declassify nuclear fusion research, marking the beginning of open intenational collaboration and shared research efforts

Engineer John D. Lawson publishes his "Criteria for a Useful Thermonuclear Reactor", stating that the product of plasma density and the energy confinement time (a measure of the rate at which energy is lost from the plasma) must be greater than a specified value for fusion to occur

1955   1957

1939   1956   »

Tritium and helium-3 from deuterium-deuterium fusion reactions directly observed for the first time at the US Berkley National Laboratory. Also, Hans Bethe publishes the first reliable theory of the fusion processes in stars

Soviet physicist Igor Kurchatov gives a lecture at Harwell (the leading research centre of the UK's Atomic Energy Research Establishment) and openly discusses nuclear fusion research, revealing for the first time that the USSR is also working on nuclear fusion

Further Reading

If you'd like to delve a bit further into some of the topics mentioned in this book (fusion or otherwise) here are some suggestions.

There are many popular science books on climate change. See, for example, *The Hot Topic* by Gabrielle Walker & David King (Bloomsbury Publishing Plc). I also like the background and history parts (chapters 1-13) of *Fixing Climate* by Kunzig & Broecker (Profile Books Ltd.). If you'd like a good summary of the science have a look at the IPCC assessment reports *Summary for Policymakers* available to view or download at www.ipcc.ch.

Significant Dates

Soviet scientists surprise the fusion community by reporting high temperatures (over 10 million degrees) on their T-3 tokamak in Moscow. A British team from Culham are invited to go and validate their measurements

Initial idea to build a joint European fusion experiment and start of design work for the Joint European Torus (JET)

1968

1971

1963

1969

UK fusion research moves from the Atomic Energy Research Establishment at Harwell to Culham Science Centre (now Culham Centre for Fusion Energy), both in Oxfordshire

The success of the mission to Moscow and the surprisingly high temperatures achieved by T-3 lead to worldwide adoption of the tokamak design for new fusion machines

For facts and figures on energy options read
Sustainability without the Hot Air by David JC
MacKay (UIT Cambridge Ltd.).

For a brief history of nuclear physics discoveries and
more on Rutherford scattering have a look at chapter
1 of *Nuclear and Particle Physics* by W.S.C. Williams
(Oxford Science Publications).

For an interesting tour of quantum physics read
Quantum Physics Cannot Hurt You by Marcus
Chown (Faber and Faber Ltd.).

If you'd like to find out more about Cold Fusion see
chapter 8 of *Fusion: Energy of the Universe* by Garry
McCracken & Peter Stott (Elsevier Academic Press).
This is also a great book if you'd like some more
technical details on both magnetic and laser fusion,
or some history and information on early fusion

The JET foundation stone
is laid at Culham Science
Centre (18th May) and
construction begins

Scientists working on the ASDEX tokamak
in Germany make a surprising discovery of
a "high confinement" mode of operation,
where turbulence at the edge of the plasma is
reduced and particle and heat confinement
is improved

1979

1982

1978

1983   »

Culham Science
Centre chosen as the
site for JET

The first JET
plasma is
made on JET
(25th June)

research. Michael Brooks also writes about cold fusion in his book *13 Things that Don't Make Sense* (Profile Books Ltd.).

For more on different types of plasmas look at *The Plasma Universe* by Curt Suplee (Cambridge University Press) or dip into the *Feynman Lectures on Physics – Volume II* by Feynman, Leighton & Sands (Addison-Wesley Publishing Company) to find out about electricity and magnetism.

Find a lot of technical information about tokamaks in the book *Tokamaks* by John Wesson (Clarendon Press) and there is a tiny bit about stellerators on the Max-Planck-Institut für Plasmaphysik website at http://tiny.cc/pkdpp.

There are in-depth brochures on JET available at www.jet.efda.org/multimedia/brochures/. Try *Focus On: JET* by Jan Mlynář and *The Science of JET* by John Wesson.

Significant Dates

Birth of the ITER project at a meeting between US President Reagan and Russian General Secretary Gorbachev, where they emphasised the importance of pursuing controlled thermonuclear fusion for peaceful purposes with international cooperation

JET is the first ever tokamak to operate using tritium (~10%)

1985

1991

1984

1987

JET's official opening ceremony takes place (9th April) attended by Her Majesty Queen Elizabeth II

Signing of the ITER agreement between the United States, the Soviet Union, the European Community and Japan. Start of initial design work

Useful Websites

GENERAL:

Culham Centre for Fusion Energy: www.ccfe.ac.uk
The Institute of Physics: www.iop.org
Fusion for Energy: fusionforenergy.europa.eu

TOKAMAKS:

All the world's tokamaks: www.tokamak.info
ITER: www.iter.org
JET: www.efda.org/jet/
Japan Atomic Energy Agency:
www-jt60.naka.jaea.go.jp/english/index-e.html
Tore Supra:
www-fusion-magnetique.cea.fr/gb/cea/ts/ts.htm

TFTR is the first tokamak to run with a 50-50 deuterium-tritium fuel mix, the optimal mix for a power station. TFTR also sees the plasma being heated by fusion alpha-particles (the helium nuclei produced in the fusion reaction)

The final design of ITER is completed. Then the USA withdraws from the project. It is decided that ITER should be scaled back to reduce costs

1993

1998

1992

1997

»

The ITER design progresses to include detailed engineering work performed by three teams in Japan, USA and Germany

JET produces world record fusion power of 16MW and Q=0.65 (Q is the ratio of fusion power produced to the external power required for plasma heating). Physicists see more clear evidence of alpha-particle heating

General Atomics (DIII-D): fusion.gat.com/global
ASDEX-Upgrade:
www.ipp.mpg.de/ippcms/eng/for/projekte/asdex
MAST: www.ccfe.ac.uk/MAST.aspx
The National Fusion Research Institute (KSTAR):
www.nfri.re.kr/english
NSTX: nstx.pppl.gov
Centre de Recherches en Physique des Plasmas
(TCV): crpp.epfl.ch
Hefei Institutes of Physical Science (EAST):
english.hf.cas.cn/r/ResearchDivisions/IPP

LASERS:

The Central Laser Facility: www.clf.rl.ac.uk
The National Ignition Facility: lasers.llnl.gov
The HiPER Project: www.hiper-laser.org

Significant Dates

The JET divertor is fully replaced
by the remote handling robots. The
European Fusion Development
Agreement (EFDA) is established to
take over responsibility for the future
use of JET

China and South Korea join
the ITER collaboration. The
USA rejoins the project

1999

2004

2001

2005

The new,
pared-down
design of
ITER is
completed

The location of the ITER site is
agreed as Cadarache, France. India
joins the collaboration

Afterword

The Institute of Physics has been running a national lecture tour for schools and colleges for at least 25 years and it has been consistently well received. The tour is aimed at 14-16 year-old students and hopes to inspire them to continue with physics post GCSE. We strive to offer a really exciting lecture with plenty of demonstrations and interactivity on a subject to capture students' imaginations and show them how their school work touches the world of ground-breaking physics research. Key to making the lecture series work is an inspiring physicist giving the talk: someone who works in (or has worked in) the area of physics they are talking about and who is a great role model. Their experience gives students a flavour of real physics and some of the careers they can aspire to if they study the subject at A level or beyond.

'Powering the Future: The Physics of Fusion' is a particularly good example of an IOP schools and colleges lecture: the research is leading-edge and the challenge of finding a sustainable energy source for

ITER agreement officially signed, creating legal entity responsible for construction, operation and decommissioning of ITER. In January, work begins on levelling the ITER site. The "Broader Approach" agreement is signed between the European Atomic Energy Community (EURATOM) and Japan, setting a framework for Japanese research in support of ITER over ten years. Design team begins preparations for DEMO as part of the Broader Approach agreement

2007

2006

2009

»

The EAST tokamak is completed in China - the first fully-superconducting tokamak (uses superconducting magnetic coils to produce both the toroidal and the poloidal magnetic fields)

The ITER platform is ready for building - 2 years were required to clear and level the 42 hectares (>100 acres, about the size of 60 football fields). Excavation work begins to explore soil and rock formation before digging the tokamak pit

the future is something which we hope will engage young people. Previous lectures have been on particle physics and the LHC, how we can use telescopes to find out more about the universe, physics and sport, and the science of light and colour. For more information on the schools and colleges lecture series and to watch past lectures online please visit www.iop.org/schoolslecture.

The schools and colleges lecture series is just one aspect of the work the Institute does to inspire students and support teachers of physics.

For students we run a membership scheme for sixth-formers, produce careers material and have recently launched an online database of physics courses for those thinking of studying physics at university.

For teachers, we provide CPD (Continuous Professional Development) opportunities through our extensive network of expert coordinators and coaches and produce a variety of teaching resources.

Significant Dates

The ground support structure for the future ITER Tokamak Complex is completed. This comprises the base mat, retaining walls and seismic plinths of the Seismic Isolation Pit - see photograph below

Digging of the first trenches on the ITER site begins. These are for pipes carrying cooling water from the Verdon river via the Canal de Provence to the cooling water tower on the ITER site

April 2010

April 2012

Sept 2011

Experiments begin on the newly-upgraded JET machine, testing the new beryllium and tungsten wall, which will be critical for ITER

We also run an affiliation scheme for schools which is a great way of keeping in touch with the Institute's Education Department and getting the latest updates about our initiatives. Membership of the scheme gives schools access to our education journal and newsletters and discounts on the courses and conferences we organise.

We also work on policy to try to preserve or improve the place of physics in schools; in particular, we are working with the government and the TDA[1] to try to increase the number of specialist physics teachers in the workforce – through recruitment, retention and CPD for non-specialists.

For more information on the work of the education department please visit www.iop.org/education.

Why do we do all this? Because we believe that a good education in physics will provide all children with something that amazes them, helps them develop intellectually and, in some cases, takes them on to a degree or career in this fascinating discipline. And, whilst many will not pursue it beyond 16, they have, at least, experienced what it is like to think like a physicist and know the satisfaction of a physics explanation.

Charles Tracy, Head of Education (pre-19), and Clare Mills, Project Coordinator, Education Team, Institute of Physics

May 2012

Planning begins for the complex logistical task of bringing large component pieces of the ITER tokamak from across three continents to the site in France

[1] TDA is the Teacher and Development Agency for Schools, since April 2012 called the Teaching Agency

Graduates from tertiary education by subject in 2009

Austria
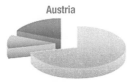

Sweden
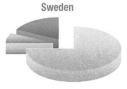

Germany

France
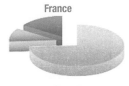

United Kingdom

Japan
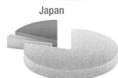

United States

Source - Eurostat

Physics, Maths, Chemistry, IT ■
Engineering ■
Other ▫